OUT OF SEQUENCE

THE SONNETS REMIXED

EDITED by D. GILSON

Parlor Press
Anderson, South Carolina
www.parlorpress.com

Parlor Press LLC, Anderson, South Carolina, 29621

© 2016 by Parlor Press. The individual works in *Out of Sequence* are published under a Creative Commons Attribution-NonCommercial-ShareAlike 4.0 International license. Individual authors retain copyright of their work.
All rights reserved.
Printed in the United States of America
S A N: 2 5 4 - 8 8 7 9

Library of Congress Cataloging-in-Publication Data

Cover Design by Christopher Cunetto.
Printed on acid-free paper.

Parlor Press, LLC is an independent publisher of scholarly and trade titles in print and multimedia formats. This book is available in paperback and ebook formats from Parlor Press on the World Wide Web at http://www.parlorpress.com or through online and brick-and-mortar bookstores. For submission information or to find out about Parlor Press publications, write to Parlor Press, 3015 Brackenberry Drive, Anderson, South Carolina, 29621, or email editor@parlorpress.com.

Contents

Introduction *xvii*
  D. Gilson

1 | **Remixed** *3*
  Jordan Stein

2 | **Sonnet Two** *4*
  Anna Maria Hong

3 | **Single** *5*
  Adam W. Clifton

4 | **Nature's Bequest: A Two-Voice Canon** *6*
  Claudia Gary

5 | **Summer's Distillation Left** *8*
  Jane Hoogestraat

6 | **Death Defier** *9*
  Stuart Barnes

7 | **Unless Thou Get a Son** *10*
  Ed Madden

8 | **A Gay Man Ponders Having Children** *11*
  Stephen S. Mills

9 | **Issueless** *12*
  Seth Pennington

10 | **Dear Doctor** *13*
  Sonja Johanson

11 | **Shaken** *14*
  Verna Kale

12 | **Sediment** *16*
  Douglas Luman

13 | **Cariad & Gwyn** *17*
  Ivy Alvarez

14 | Fourteen *18*
Leah Brennan

15 | Engraft *19*
Michele Seminara

16 | Hymn for Atlanta *20*
Peter LaBerge

17 | If Only I Could Sing *21*
Barbra Nightingale

18 | Beginning Without a Question *22*
Susan Grimm

19 | The Phoenix and the Lion: A Hauntology *23*
Patrick Thomas Henry

20 | Upon Finding Online a ".jpg" Copy of the Newly Authenticated Portrait of Shakespeare by John Sanders *25*
A. W. Strouse

21 | Erroneousness at Its Finest *26*
Haley Searls

22 | Heart Swap Ward *28*
Cameron Hunt McNabb

23 | Hyperbole *29*
Randall Mann

24 | Mine eye hath play'd the painter and hath stell'd *30*
Ellen McGrath Smith

25 | Fragment of Joan *31*
Rachel Danielle Peterson

26 | Pick Up the Nearest Book to You, Turn to Page 45. The Second Sentence Explains Your Love Life *33*
Michael D. Snediker

Contents

27 | Sleep Apnea   *34*
   Maia Gil'Adi

28 | The Temporary Rot of Insomnia   *35*
   Sarah Grodzinski

29 | Outcast Ballad   *36*
   Jason Roush

30 | Waste Then   *37*
   Robert Whitehead

31 | Reverence from an Irreverent Catholic   *38*
   Michael Slattery

32 | Night Find   *40*
   Tanya Camp

33 | Sunstroke   *41*
   Andrea Janelle Dickens

34 | Trinity   *42*
   Ann Cefola

35 | Wat Mahatat   *43*
   Jeff Streeby

36 | Farm Boys   *44*
   Talin Tahajian

37 | Sonnet 37   *45*
   Alexandra Reisner

38 | April Flowered Skies   *48*
   Robert Darcy

39 | Zozzled   *49*
   Lynn Schmeidler

40 | Slaughter in Three Parts   *50*
   Bryan Borland

41 | Pretty Wrongs   *51*
   Lanette Cadle

42 | Bend Dexter   *52*
    Michael Flory

43 | Dark as Light   *53*
    Beth Gylys

44 | Cage Me   *54*
    Zack Rosen

45| On Reading Shakespeare #45 and Orwell's *Wigan Pier* in the Same Late Afternoon Light   *55*
    Edward Bevan

46 | House of Pain   *56*
    Jeffery Berg

47 | So Who Am I When I'm with You   *61*
    Ana Garza G'z

48 | Supermarket in Brooklyn   *62*
    Maria Schurr

49 | Succulent   *63*
    Carol Dorf

50 | Sonnet 50 on Coosa River Banks   *64*
    Bo McGuire

51 | Lovers Misread Envy Horses Homonyms   *65*
    Kendra Leonard

52 | Free Market   *67*
    Elizabeth Thompson

53 | Every (blessed) Shape We Know   *68*
    Rita Cotera

54 | again, we garden the increase we want prolonged   *69*
    RJ Gibson

55 | The Assembly   *70*
    Terry Belew

56 | eat the rich / the rectum is a grave   *71*
   Theodora Danylevich

57 | Pressing Love   *72*
   Bonnie S. Kaplan

58 | At Your Hand   *73*
   Sylvia Sukop

59 | If This be Form, Then Let This Not be From   *74*
   Gretchen E. Henderson

60 | Vestige   *75*
   Christopher Kempf

61 | The Watchman   *77*
   Krystal Marsh

62 | Selfie: I'm   *78*
   Aaron DeLee

63 | Drawn Lines   *79*
   Robert Adams

64 | Defaced   *80*
   Mario DiGangi

65 | The One in Which We Outwit Time   *81*
   Donna Vorreyer

66 | Tired for Rest   *82*
   Winston H. Plowes

67 | Shadow Rose   *83*
   Natalie Byers

68 | Running for Town Alderman   *85*
   C. Russell Price

69 | Although Their Eyes Were Kind   *86*
   Kelly McQuain

70 | Busted Sonnet to the Muse   *87*
    Christopher Crawford

71 | Hospital Visit   *88*
    Wendy Bashant

72 | Lest the World   *90*
    Thomas Magnussen and Bjørn Palmqvist

73 | Balancing Act   *91*
    David McAleavey

74 | Perfect-Perverse   *92*
    Tom La Farge

75 | The Full Deck   *93*
    Mark Ward

76 | One Foot After the Other   *94*
    K. Tyler Christiansen

77 | A Primer   *96*
    Pamela Johnson Parker

78 | A Drag Queen Writes to William Shakespeare   *97*
    Michael Carosone

79 | The Changeful Muse   *99*
    Heather Ladd

80 | Roadside Boy   *107*
    Paul O'Brien

81 | Two Headstones   *108*
    Sara Button

82 | Muse, Gross Painting   *109*
    Grant Metzker

83 | Wagon   *110*
    Samuel R. Yates

84 | Facsimile   *111*
    Benjamin Steiner

85 | Under the Photo of Koo Koo the Bird Girl, I Let You Inside of Me   *112*
    Vincent James Trimboli

86 | With Will, Breakfast at Waffle House   *114*
    Joshua Peter Kulseth

87 | The Poem That Should Not Exist   *116*
    Jonathan Hsy

88 | Story of Faults Concealed   *118*
    Christine Swint

89 | Banister   *119*
    Jack Kahn

90 | Ars Poetica   *121*
    Louis Maraj

91 | Love Poem for Modest Three-Bedroom Ranch   *122*
    Jim Daniels

92 | Cutup Will   *123*
    Wendy Walker

93 | The System   *125*
    Jessica Server

94 | Aug. 15th for William Shakespeare   *130*
    Eléna Rivera

95 | Endnotes   *131*
    Dustin Brookshire

96 | The Wanton Youth to his Forty-Six-Year-Old Boyfriend   *132*
    Michael Walsh

97 | Winter Absence   *133*
    Jay Stevenson

98 | Absent, Dressed, Trim   *134*
   Julie Houchens

99 | Froward Violet   *135*
   Sujata Iyengar

100 | Un-a-mused   *136*
   Carlton D. Fisher

101 | Truant Muse   *137*
   Kelly Jones

102 | Sweets Grown Common   *138*
   Niamh J. O'Leary

103 | Dulling My Lines, and Doing Me Disgrace   *139*
   RJ Ingram

104 | For Fear   *140*
   Beth Ayer

105 | Buger, $, Wifi: Fair, Kind, and True   *141*
   Julian Modugno

106 | Neuer before Imprinted   *142*
   Linday Ann Reid

107 | Dream Journal: Train Ride   *143*
   Kathy Gilbert

108 | Remorse Re-Morsed   *144*
   John J. Trause

109 | Rorschach Keeps Watch   *145*
   Paul Strohm

110 | The Paul Simon Annotations, or, You Can Call Me Sonnet 110   *146*
   Ari Friedlander

111 | Eisel   *148*
   David B. Goldstein

112 | To O'ergreen Abysm   *151*
   Rachel Levens

113 | Mine Eye Untrue   *152*
   Brad Clompus

114 | Bathroom Selfie: every bad a perfect best   *154*
   Kinsley Stocum

115 | Let's Never Have It All   *155*
   Randolph Pfaff

116 | Old Love   *156*
   Cathleen Calbert

117 | Sonnet CVII + 7   *157*
   Martin Elwell

118 | Andy Warhol, Sonnet CXVIII   *158*
   Em Ruiz

119 | The Castro, 1986   *159*
   Alison Powell

120 | Because they say honesty is the best policy, but anyway who are they to say anything at all   *160*
   Wythe Marschall

121 | The Eleven Revere the Letter 'e,' Remember the Twelfth   *162*
   Erik Schurink

122 | Gifts   *163*
   Theodora Ziolkowski

123 | The Happiest You've Ever Been   *164*
   Sarah Rubin

124 | My Dear Love Erasure   *165*
   Jordan Windholz

125 | Until   *166*
   Claude Clayton Smith

126 | Sonnet 126 Remix   *167*
   Matthew Hittinger

127 | Dark Ladies at the Magazine Stand   *168*
   Jennifer Perrine

128 | Haiku for the Pianist   *169*
   Tom Merrill

129 | 129   *170*
   Jehanne Dubrow

130 | 1:30 am, Spoken in the Backseat of a Souped-up Sunbird   *171*
   Antonio Vallone

131 | Power Without Face   *172*
   Sarah Leavens

132 | Two-in-the-Morning Eyes   *173*
   Eric Hack

133 | Prison Moan & Mistranslation   *174*
   Angelo Pastormerlo

134 | Trinity   *175*
   William Reichard

135 | Stage Directions   *176*
   D. Gilson

136 | My Name Is Will   *178*
   Will Stockton

137 | Little Monster   *179*
   Michael Basinski

138 | Bar Napkin Bouts-Rimés   *181*
   Moria Egan

139 | Birthday Sonnet (Second Verse)   *182*
   Mark Cugini

140 | My Pity-Wanting Pain: A Tonka Tale   *183*
   Neal Whitman

141 | Proud Heart's Slave   *185*
   Daniel Zender

142 | Before the Tribulation   *186*
   Maggie O'Connor

143 | Euphemism and Taxonomy: Wild Domestic Birds   *187*
   Alexandra Edelblute

144 | Ackuna's Bad Translator   *189*
   Ross McCleary

145 | Re: CXLV   *190*
   Andy Decker

146 | When My Mother Calls Me Thin   *191*
   Caroline Tanski

147 | Weak Constitution   *192*
   Lisa Ampleman

148 | Mine Eye   *193*
   Dianne Berg

149 | Sinew is a Thing We Have Uses For   *194*
   Chris Emslie

150 | Still Life with Unrequited Love   *195*
   Jennifer Franklin

151 | Conscious Young, Body Treason   *196*
   Kevin Barton

152 | Here & Not Here: New Love Bearings   *197*
   Jennifer Murvin

153 | Sonnet 153 while you were sleeping   *210*
   Pamela Allen Brown

154 | I Don't Understand Shakespeare's Sonnet #154   *211*
   Wayne Koestenbaum

Afterword | Remixing as Performance   *213*
   Ayanna Thompson

Contributors   *217*

About the Editor   *243*

Introduction

D. Gilson

"That thus our everyday might never die," Jordan Stein opines in the first entry to this collection, an echoing of not only Shakespeare, certainly himself consumed with (im)mortality, but also the 1984 hit single "Forever Young" by German pop group Alphaville. The latter has been covered and remixed many times over, used in films like *Napoleon Dynamite*, television shows like *Queer as Folk*, and commercials for Saturn and McDonald's. And though we have many deliberate reinventions of Shakespeare's plays—my favorite among them 1999's *10 Things I Hate About You*, an adaptation of *The Taming of the Shrew* staring a swoon-worthy Heath Ledger—we have decidedly fewer of his poetry.

It is easy to imagine many of us as subconsciously influenced by Shakespeare's *Sonnets* in our own work; we find in these 154 "events" that which has consumed us long before their writing and long after: love and sex and death, bodies and birth and decay, the extraordinary and the everyday. Conversely, Freud describes consciousness as a "highly fugitive condition," one which I welcomed contributors to more aptly explore in *Out of Sequence: The Sonnets Remixed*. If Shakespeare the auteur and his sonnets have influenced so much of how we think (and act) as humans, how might we be un- and redone by the conscious act of responding to (or through) these seventeenth century verses? Here you will find a wide variety of remixes; entries various by their form—poems, short essays, comics, songs, and art; and various by their remixer—poets, essayists, artists, musicians, and scholars. As such, I imagine these pages as a type of queer utopia, a place where things and people touch, though they are too often taught not to.

As both a poet and scholar interested in affect, I was most interested in editing this collection as a way of exploring how in a specific moment—today, the second decade of the twenty-first century—we might remix the most famous poetic sequence of all time, William Shakespeare's *The Sonnets*, a sequence which constantly renders us obsessed with the past, yet out of order, misreading, responding, remixing. The submissions we received surprised me by not only their artistic value, but also their theoretical optimism. In responding to sonnet five, Jane Hoogestraat describes "a corner of the heart where summer / is always ending, but never quite." Though in 97 we find the poet "dreading the winter's near," Jay Stevenson's corresponding photograph renders the coming season a time when one may lounge in the bath, sip something warm, and be reborn. Even in the face of pandemic, like the AIDS-stricken Castro of 1986 which Alison Powell describes in remixing 119, we find ourselves returning to a pruned city, yes, but "welcomed / by the strong backs of a thousand orphaned horses, / a few kind widows who will have unmarked the doors." Shakespeare wrote poems and plays before theory was a conscious act; and yet, what we find in his *Sonnets* allows for our own creative and critical work to meander not as separate, but coexistent, endeavors.

It has been an honor to curate the entries found in these pages. I must thank not only the 154 remixers, but also Ayanna Thompson for her beautiful afterword and generous mentorship. Additionally, thank you to the Department of English at The George Washington University for its support of me and for providing a home to queer exploration; thank you especially to Jeffrey Jerome Cohen, Holly Dugan, Jonathan Hsy, Alexa Huang, Connie Kiebler, Tony López, Robert McRuer, and Gayle Wald. This collection would not exist without the tireless efforts of and brotherly love given me by Will Stockton, whose remixes of scholarship and poetry not only inspire me constantly, but also make me a deeper, more creative thinker. I hope you enjoy the artifacts you find here, and that they inspire you to your own remixes in thought and on page.

OUT OF SEQUENCE

1 | Remixed

Jordan Stein

From all our social media we desire increase,
That thus our everyday might never die,
And as clever quips by time become mere set-piece
Re-perusal can inspire creativity:
Reblogged memes the iPhone amplifies,
Feed'st Facebook's feed with self-substantial fuel,
Hashtagging every picture where #nofilter lies,
And tweeting all thy foes, with thy sweet tweet too cruel:
Reply we now with but a fresh emoticon
And rejoice when we live-blog any foolish thing,
For to awake, arise, and quickly to log on
Is to be right now, and to be right now is king.
So pity not when you click "like" on my selfie,
Lest you make us spell the word aloud, "O-M-G."

2 | Sonnet Two

Anna Maria Hong

Pumped as a golden animal or
breast full of dark light
mineral, let the furrow
of forty winters

lapse. For a season,
did I wax
the tallow. Let
the wane begin.

For forty summers too,
did I hie
my prime and hem
my love to

those zones above and fix
my star.

3 | Single

Adam W. Clifton

4 | Nature's Bequest: A Two-Voice Canon

Claudia Gary

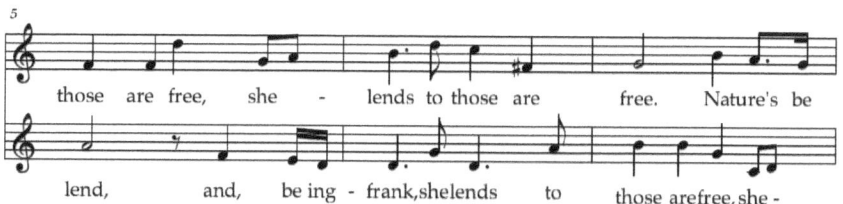

A Note on the Music

"Nature's Bequest" is a very brief vocal setting of lines 3 and 4 of Shakespeare's Sonnet 4. I wrote this two-voice canon in 1981 while taking a course in musical composition. The course's goal was to create a foundation for composing polyphonic music.

This particular assignment, based on one of the lessons J.S. Bach taught to his students, was to choose a short excerpt from any Shakespeare sonnet and create a two-part canon. An additional goal was that the music be meaningfully related to the poem. I chose to do this by using the word "lend" (in Sonnet 4, line 3) as a take-off point for Voice 2 of the canon. The word acquires an extra layer of meaning as it describes the process of a musical canon, in which one voice branches to become two or more.

In this notation and recording of the canon, the second voice has several notes transposed upward by an octave to enable a soprano to sing both lines. The two vocal lines are otherwise basically equivalent.

5 | Summer's Distillation Left

Jane Hoogestraat

There is a corner of the heart where summer
is always ending, but never quite—an August evening
preserved, Dickinson's guest that would be gone,
a courteous yet harrowing grace, the last bright
gladiolus blooming, the brittle lawn reseeded,
landscape being pared down, bearing that
spare look of a sadness without cause, a litany
of sameness in the days to come between the sheaves
in golden light and the driving winds of yesteryear.
Take any season that you like, and what remains
will be cordial enough, if you have been careful
in your loves, they with you. Such endings we prepare
for when time seems kind, such choices we make.

6 | Death Defier

Stuart Barnes

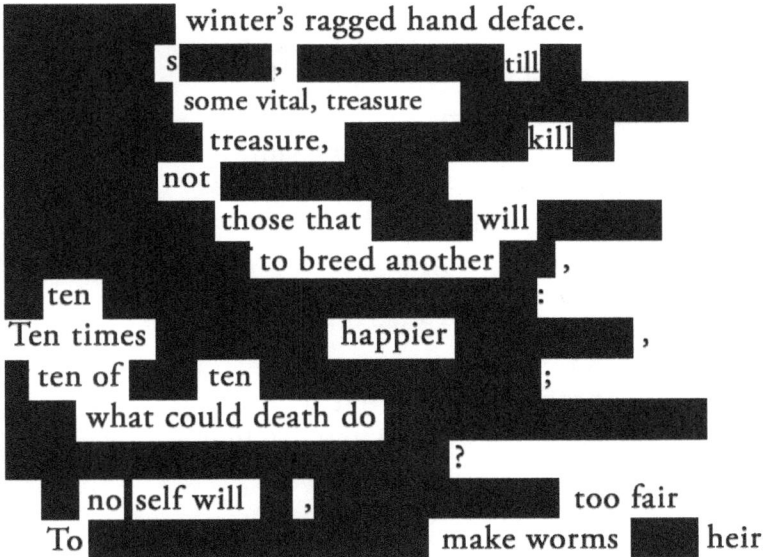

7 | Unless Thou Get a Son

Ed Madden

My dad was god, got up with dawn to start
the day. His word was firm, his hand, too,
on my shoulder, his love. Those days, we stopped
our work for lunch sometime after noon,
men and boys around my grandma's table—
ham and beans, tomatoes, tea, the sun
leaned in the window. Summer days
grew long, longer, the work went well past dusk.
The heat never broke despite the dark.
Tractor lights burned red and white, made laps
across the field. I watched for the truck
coming down the rows to pick me up—
my dad, my brother, some hired hands, a water
jug, and after, the long ride home together.

8 | A Gay Man Ponders Having Children

Stephen S. Mills

Someone just tweeted another picture
of Neil Patrick Harris and his damn babies,
which makes your phantom ovaries ache
and makes me reach for my bottle of gin,
which I will drink throughout the night,
loving everything bad for me. In a drunken
stupor, I'll imagine us as daddies: fancy
stroller parading down the streets of Harlem
like gay movie stars. We'd be much less
threatening with babies instead of our
normal strut with a third linked in our arms:
a man wanting us to make him our boy toy.
Yes, I've been the daddy to many men,
which will only increase the older I get.
But actual infants are so time consuming,
and I like the music we make just the two
of us. Our strings rubbing together in perfect
harmony. You and me: childless men who
know it's the bad things that make the life.

9 | Issueless

Seth Pennington

Mother's breathing fear
of losing, her loss, what really was
lost in the foil of river and Chevrolet
crimping first son's lungs, quiets now twenty
years after, after lasting son sings his choice to
widow every woman he once promised, sings
to a man with a soft jaw and slight shoulder
he calls home. Mother answers gravely; she's grown
accustomed to feral cats more than people.
Always she begins, *Why not have a woman, for
the chance?* Mother stops to breathe, sniffs, is
curbed and tied with the news of two fathers,
listens for small feet crunching leaf or snow piles,
and like a burial vault flooded, pushed to surface, a
smile.

10 | Dear Doctor

Sonja Johanson

Deny it if you want to—
you've made an art of dodging
grants, playing shrink for all
the ladies. There's no evidence
of your costumes, that possessive
box, the degrees you've sought
and stuck on your jacket,
hoping to prove a ruined hero.

Don't you think this act is getting
old? Aren't you a little ashamed
to live here still? Change it up. Be
tough. Not to say that you have to
stop drinking, but damn, handsome,
slow down. Make the world a mirror.

11 | Shaken

Verna Kale

On August 23, 2011, an earthquake near Mineral, Virginia, damaged the Washington Monument, closing it indefinitely. Forty miles from the epicenter I felt the tremors as I was sitting on the OB-GYN's examination table in a backless gown and sock feet, cold inside and out. I thought at first that the shaking was a truck rolling by outside, but in the five-story brick hospital building the rumbles went on and on.

"Are we having an earthquake?" I asked the doctor. I had held a monopoly on all the fear and uncertainty in the room, but with the walls and floor and ceiling shaking, we were suddenly and equally helpless. "I think we are," she said. Then she disappeared into the hall. For a few seconds I noted the indignity of dying half-naked in a hospital gown, though, thinking about it now, I guess that's actually the norm.

We sometimes say of an experience that makes us confront some harsh reality—mortality, loss, truth—"I was shaken." Forty seconds earlier the doctor had told me that I would need surgery to find out why my body was refusing to let me stay pregnant. Then the plates of the earth's crust shifted.

When the shaking stopped, I felt neither frightened nor relieved. The mass of tissue inside me was no longer alive, but I was, and at least there's that. Equilibrium had returned. My world had been rocked and set to rights.

Medical records refer to miscarriage as "spontaneous abortion," a choice of words so at odds with the intense desire to grow a life that the patient questions whether she's been given the right file. An early miscarriage is called a "chemical pregnancy," or, if the pregnancy progressed a bit further, a "blighted ovum." The former suggests that you were never really pregnant; the latter implies that your body produced a dud, something that should not be. Then they send you home to wait it out, which you do, alone.

Shakespeare's suggestion that we should *Let those whom nature hath not made for store, / Harsh, featureless, and rude, barrenly perish* stings the woman who has experienced pregnancy loss or infertility. Thank goodness for the turn, which shakes us up and puts things right!

While the beautiful and bounteous re-populate the world with copies of their younger, better selves, there remains another way to outlast this perilous, shifting existence—a way less beholden to the vagaries of Nature's fickle generosities. A text, too, is a copy of the self - conceived in passion, painfully born, nurtured, and sent out to make its own way in the world. Publish or perish: *herein lives wisdom, beauty, and increase.*

12 | Sediment

Douglas Luman

Gather your grit, feinting the barbs
       of need, seasoned serenades of prose & roses,
             tide seeping tar. You are the rime of an egret,
heart trekking high above the trees, a feather form
       finding freer math of the map above that tin pool
           where lilacs wilt, serene ferns stir
& words are drawn as arrows, not wards, bathing
       like rattlers in the rays of the sun. You are not
            grist for the mill. Not straw which burns
carmine, the color of ire,
       but an eagle from an eggshell –
           wild against a cobalt sky.

13 | Cariad & Gwyn

Ivy Alvarez

Are the waves approaching presaging a storm? Let's prepare
live samphire, waving sages, storm drains filling doubtless give
lease of dull sapphire weaving, sagacious doubts soon decrease.
Werewolves hold woven breaths, grace us sooner, a dullard bear.
Decay and rancour left out bodily, give out warnings, creak
 boards all day,

uphold the roof of graceless ruin, a foreboding. Something falls,
 warns of swaying cold.
Know the papers, words left outside its walls, and so and so . . .
Pluck the bare, the woven, falling jester and cloven-hoofed, the
 faceless luck,
astronomy, fallen portents, dullish fires of countless quality.

Tell me a story, I ask him, tell it stormy, dark and well.
Wind the yarn around your finger, you'll pull me in, you'll find.
Derive no breathless pleasure, or wine, or castaway, or tales to
 thrive.
Art is a colour in your eye. He smiles and writes it down. From
 air convert,
prognosticate, decide. Drink your stout. We'll go out, sweet
 propitious date.

14 | Fourteen

Leah Brennan

wife and wife seek a man
in nature worthy of increase
father for copy

drawn like the knight of cups
red cloaked, riding bridled white horse
chalice in hand, seed to store

shuffled through lovers, the moon,
the fool, pages and judgment,
the world from inconstant stars

15 | Engraft

Michele Seminara

Man is conceived upon this sullied stage
and like a seedling grows, but then decreases.
He vaunts his youthful sap in brave conceit,
till wasteful time decays his day to night.

Everything holds but a little moment—
even your perfection cannot stay.
So I'll make war with time and as he takes you,
make love, and with my pen engraft you new.

16 | Hymn for Atlanta

Peter LaBerge

Quiet, the toaster. Quiet, the scalloped flesh,
the bathroom sinks. Saints wander the boy's head

like men lost in hallways, like children watching
mothers mop violent mornings into nightgowns.

The wisdom of Georgia is spread wide across
duplex floors—boys white as scarecrows

long-bleached and convinced they are men,
boys willing to piece together the broken

weathervanes of foreclosing farms, maiden
gardens. This boy is left with his mother white

as fox underbelly, a consolation
prize of blessed skin, of rivers and begonias.

17 | If Only I Could Sing

Barbra Nightingale

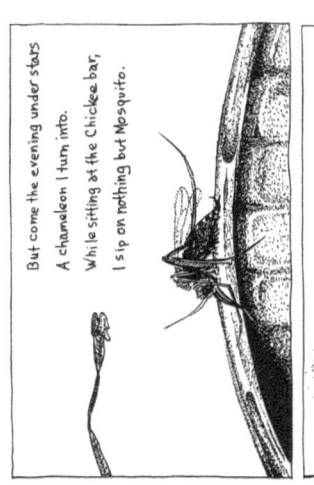

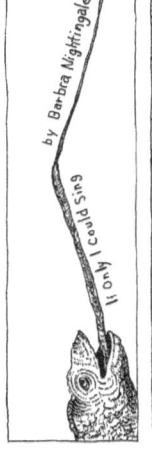
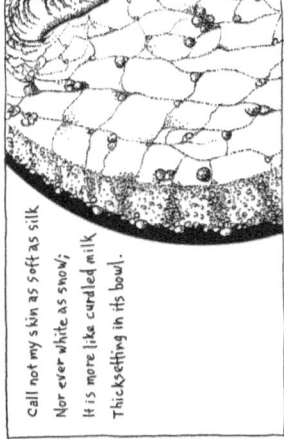
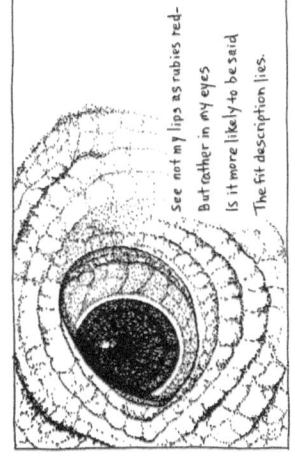

18 | Beginning Without a Question

Susan Grimm

When I pinned your blue eye. When I collected
my sweat in a jar. When I fingered the scabs

of my knees like a phrenologist. Was it
summer, some wind. Handsome meant

easy to handle then. I was so pliant
there was no plaint yet. Sometime

long ago. So long it became a way to say
goodbye. Clover chains—they cannot

hold you. A frolic of grass. Some wind
meddlesome in your hair. When you toss

back your head. The sun and trees quarrel-
some. The wind a lisping of invisible stars.

19 | The Phoenix and the Lion: A Hauntology
After Jacques Derrida after William Shakespeare

Patrick Thomas Henry

[The time]

when the slope-shouldered lion, triumphant, lurks through
the leonine yellow of wind-fanned, sun-withered grass
with his white incisors piercing, prizing the phoenix by
the bird's fractured spine; convulsing, she molts embers
of feathers and blood that, glowing, cascade to blunted
brown earth where they cinder, cool, spend themselves
in desperate grey moans of smoke that gather until destiny
blows them onward, in pursuit of the lion's black-fanged
hunting shadow. That shadow, ghost of devouring time,

[is out]

staging for the end of history, when the lion's hour will come:
after rending the phoenix with age-blunted claws, after the long-
lived phoenix's blood burns centuries away in his gullet and
renders inside him sulfurous and tormenting flames. Poor lion,
poor ghost: encountering the phoenix, the first time is always
a last time. So do whatever you will, Time: but you shall do
your worst. What the lion and the phoenix unfold, I bound
myself to hear, and to revenge: to witness the heat emanating
from the cinders hatching—beak and feathers flaring forth -
in a nest of leonine yellow grass; to witness in the emerald of a
lion's eyes a phoenix's thousand lives immolating his psyche.
This, Time, is what you seek to scratch out in dark lines that
spill black and blood-hot from the nib of your antique pen—
Time devours all: lion and phoenix—but the story phases, out

[of joint]

in uncoupled chains of wild and whirling words that evoke the advent of their (of our) silent ghosts. Phoenix, love, may the beauty in this pattern of fire-born lines uncouple us from Time's hell. Phoenix: though my verse apprises you not of eternal youth, it can fashion in the forge of your revivals links, words of eternal reprisal. Rest, rest, perturbed spirit: we will go on together, fingers sealing our lips. You, phoenix, rise from the silences to rekindle the faint fires of memory, against Time, cooling us instant old as raked coals. You and I were reborn to set this right. So come, let's go together.

20 | Upon Finding Online a ".jpg" Copy of the Newly Authenticated Portrait of Shakespeare by John Sanders

A. W. Strouse

I still can't see his face that nature painted,
for how may oils master, express his passion?
How the photo of that painting? Not acquainted
with him are copied copied copies now in fashion.
Not onto warmth of living breast I snuggle,
but close, to the screen of my computer
where flat on flat makes flat; here depth must struggle
the globe into a circle. The suitor
of nature, the illusion that pursues her,
is made of her, consumes her; it falsifies:
the ghost of carbon's date may misconstrue her,
make her stale and flat, so she herself tells lies.
      Then why should I have need to see his visage?
      There is no truth if truth is but an image.

21 | Erroneousness at Its Finest

Haley Searls

Look! Can you not measure his beauty
without comparison? Is there anything more true
than what is looking you in the eye? I write
for my beloved, and myself. That is the only purpose.
When you boast at the expense of love
no praise should be given more than need be.

This is your declaration: *Although I am physically unable to be
by your side, I am consciously aware that your beauty
surpasses all other things. I am entirely in love
with every aspect of you. Your voice, speaks true*
locutions of gold with each phrase saturated with purpose.
There is nothing, nothing in this world that I could write

*About, that would explain to any creature the right
amount of splendor you possess. If you were to be
a flower, your fragrance would serve no other purpose
than to be inhaled by the gods, and the twinkling beauty
of your eyes would light their heavens. What I say is true.*
Again, that is your proclamation, of your love.

Now I will tell you how I, a person feeling genuine love
would define my beloved. I would only ever write
about my love in a way that illustrated his beauty to be true.
Even though my adoration spreads past the Earth's end, my
    darling will only be
equated to any other human being. His eyes will light mine
    with their beauty
but not as bright as the stars light the universe. As a flower, the
    purpose

Of his aroma will be for me, and for me alone to breathe.
   For the purpose
of breathing is to give life, and my life is my love.
I will not, and cannot truthfully compare the beauty
of my treasure to the treasure that authors write
about in a privateer novel. For that would be
an exaggeration, and naturally un-true.

A comparison of my love that would be true,
would actually be no comparison at all, but a statement,
   whose purpose
would serve none other than to indicate how my darling
   should be
defined. You should not relate your one-and-only love
to one or more objects that are far beyond comparison.
   But write
with integrity about the simplicity of his beauty.

Because what I am experiencing is nothing more than
   true love,
I cannot tolerate those, whose purpose is to write
About, and be pretentious with, their beloved's beauty.

22 | Heart Swap Ward

Cameron Hunt McNabb

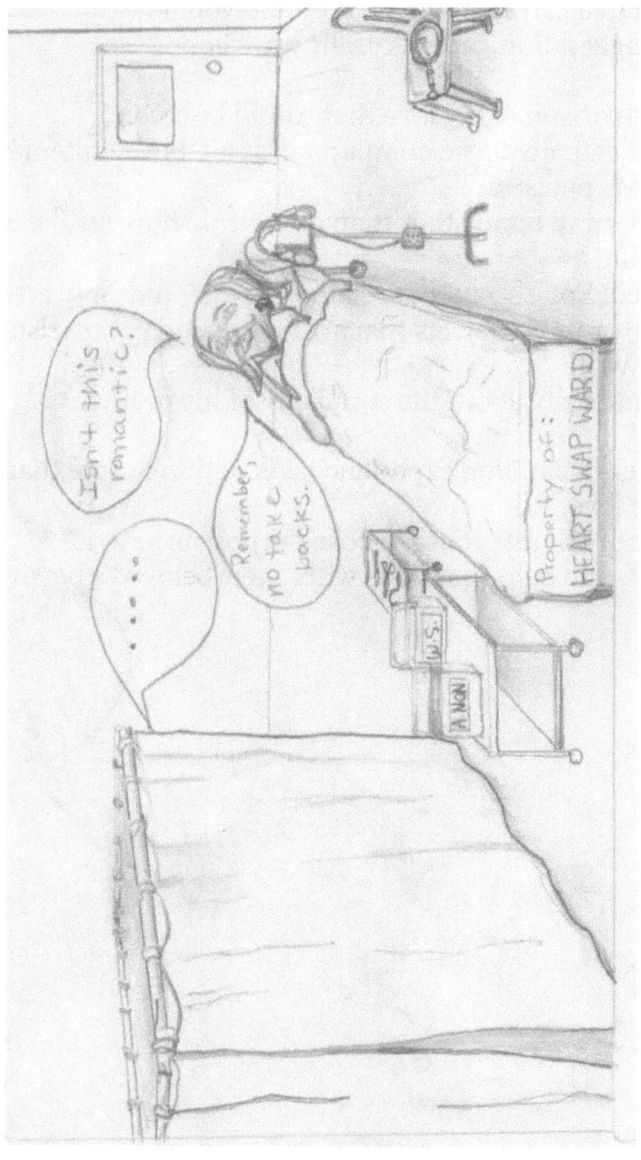

Illustrated by Bryan Kummerdelete

23 | Hyperbole

Randall Mann

I start with good intentions. On a date,
I struggle not to sound so insincere;
I think, hyperbole will be my fate.

Last night I found a fairly decent mate.
When cruising for a partner on the pier,
I start with good intentions, on a date.

Last night was filled with ways to fabricate
affection: tulips; lube; imported beer,
I think. Hyperbole will be my fate:

I left before he might reciprocate;
I swallowed so his mother wouldn't hear.
I start with good intentions on a date -

my upswept hair; my briefs. I'm losing weight.
What stays, like some insipid trick, is fear.

24 | Mine eye hath play'd the painter and hath stell'd

Ellen McGrath Smith

She was bent over blonde when she said to the mirror
which, being a mirror, was me, "Know what's funny?"

That's the butternut squash turning in on itself,
a crooked finger inviting despondent types in

to a mealy and damp early fall. Nostradamus
and his yellow horde came out of the taxi cab's

battered exhaust. I speak and you speak, we all speak
for aspic, and dreaming, somebody in the eighties

named Sasha spoons quaking kholodets onto my palms.
"How most people think we won the Cold War, the U.S."

Someone flushes, someone hollers "If it's yellow, let it
  mellow."
Call this painting *CyberRestroom, twenty-thirteen*. Like
  it twice.

25 | Fragment of Joan

Rachel Danielle Peterson

. . . Confess? It's easy to catch man's middle.
When he gazes, sees God Behind her eyes,
that he'll truss. Every time. Shorn anew, I heed
metal as you doff violet seems. Obscure, it is, skin
beneath small-clothes and trousers that decide robes,
or armor, what raiment. Who owns the pride
from such mastery of stitches? Not the stitcher
nor her sons possess the holey, stained shift beneath
all gear and trim, what nuns discovered when they
stripped : lice, maiden-head pried out by their long,
probing fingernails, horns, I say. Goat, ewe, you'll
savage with each bleat, drum, of honest heresy.
Give me the cups. My lips fill this chalice,
taste sweet brandy-wine. I am a vessel of blood,
sup deepest when snot-mouthes, gorged,
they think me kind, and Communion will bind
bride and groom with celestial linen, yet I'll
yoke you to such Friction. You blush, sir.
Take the cups! What need I for wine? There?
Hear that? The drums come for me like thunder.
I see you through water . . . maybe? Who can tell
what the rain will wash. Fear my pelt, Sir!
The soul is always some virgin that limbers
your holy even when her thighs startle like
wild squab. Tender or insatiable, your pry
toward Eternity, to stave off Death, will fail.
So blanch like drowned eels in heat, I
won't deny that Heavenly, helmed, Trumpeter,
heedless of the colour. Visages Burnished, Awful,
Stricken, Horned are The Faces, The Lord.
They hate you worse than a younger sibling,

a child-less rut. Me? the worst of it. Secret Eye.
Can't touch even if you cry, O Terrible Muse!
How could I leave you to tremble, to hobble
through each pastoral scene? Doterring fool,
here She stands, your Mother and your Maid.
Vengeful Muse. God Beneath You. Sing Me.
I'll know you by your lilt, your tongue, *To The Virgin*!
To Her Sword! I'll loosen My Breath, friends,
torch every goddamn skirt in England—

26 | Pick Up the Nearest Book to You, Turn to Page 45. The Second Sentence Explains Your Love Life

Michael D. Snediker

One can only judge on the facts.
And yet I can read you with rapture.
It forms a net so slack that everything slips
through. All things unto our flesh are kind.
You can hold a coin in your hand and yet
not touch its value. Where we think
we have words, "a virtual trail of fires"
shoots through us. The fields are rotting
as the ice lets go. Look in the hundreds
of persons that each of us knows.
The Essential Cause of the Itch appears
to be a Vast Number of Minute Animals.
He was a lucky fox that left his tail in the trap.
Please don't let on that I wrote to you.

[Thomas James, *Letters to a Stranger*, no page 45]
[Leo Bersani, *The Forms of Violence*, no page 45]
[Claudia Rankine, *Don't Let Me be Lonely*, no page 45]

27 | Sleep Apnea

Maia Gil'Adi

> Lo! thus, by day my limbs, by night my mind,
> For thee, and for myself, no quiet find.
>
> —*Sonnet 27*

It is hard to remember now. But if you think about the cases it will bring the image of the boy. The one who lived next door that summer you were seven or eight. The one who collected butterflies. Look at the cases. There are multicolored butterflies in them. A pin holds each through the middle, their wings spread, showing symmetrical patterns. They are so quiet and delicate and almost translucent behind the glass. You let your face get close to them. These are his, the boy's. He must have been older. He already knew how to play the violin. You climb the brick wall in the early morning on Sundays. You spend the day together playing in the garden, lying in the hammock, touching feet. You take the steps in-two to his room. You open the door with care. There are butterflies in cases here too. His gaze is tender toward them, hushed. They are so delicate and paper-thin. You wonder how it would feel to be that fragile; so fine and easy to break. Turn, turn this way, you would think. His face so close to the butterflies he could almost kiss them.

28 | The Temporary Rot of Insomnia

Sarah Grodzinski

Your plastic cupid skin was once refreshing,
your temples glowed gold.
Now the moonlight and the sharpness
of the changing seasons
washes them away.
I crave the flannel sheets of my bed
to retire the throb
of my unquiet mind.
It stirs me from sleep
and glues my eyes to the ceiling
to stare in agony at the stains
made from the rainwater
which leaks through my roof.
I make out a picture of a cat,
of a woman on a rocking chair.
You, my presenter of scorn, presenter of merit,
turn me into a reckless wanderer
when all I crave is to break
consciousness as the pores of the evening
slowly drain.

29 | Outcast Ballad

Jason Roush

Despair is mostly silent,
heard only inwardly,

and desolation's always
more interesting than love.

Fortune belongs to others.
Longing to be them: the worst

of curses. Though despair
is also honest and spares one

that lame and tiresome game
of lining up the right lines.

Let the faces of passers-by
remain as far removed

as the ceiling of the sky.
Love will not appear

before or after the volta.

30 | Waste Then

Robert Whitehead

There is unmovable violet   in the wet electric eye   Widowhood consuming the only
apprehension of your loss O   if the impossible would die   if your beauty would reply
As an incessant warfare   the world would widow still   A weeping as public as the
mind when your beauty left   When every hand is unable   to touch the young man's mind
Specifically, what shall not pass   is everything springlike   The world shifts vastly
To destroy its position   End to lake end   No love invincible   No blood-sense of shame

31 | Reverence from an Irreverent Catholic

Michael Slattery

> A person once asked me, in a provocative manner, if I approved of homosexuality. I replied with another question: "Tell me: when God looks at a gay person, does he endorse the existence of this person with love, or reject and condemn this person?" We must always consider the person.
>
> – *Pope Francis*

[How many a holy and obsequious tear]

2013. Thunderstruck when I read this declaration from the current Bishop of Rome, Pope Francis. Amazed that I was witnessing a change in attitude from Church leadership. "Radical" statements about homosexuality, blessings to people with facial deformities, washing the feet of Muslim women in a Holy Thursday ritual; the newest pope's message seemed to be one long disregarded by the Catholic Church: "We must always consider the person."

[Hath dear religious love stol'n from mine eye]

I was brought up Irish Catholic. Every Christmas, Lent, and Easter, we attended church promptly. Passive guilt other Sundays for shirking. I was baptized, catechized, communionized, and confirmationized. Always, unease over the lessons that I was learning, with mounting rules. By confirmation, I knew I was gay. I was sin. On the news, Pope Benedict IX called homosexuality an "objectively disordered inclination" with "enormous consequences on a variety of levels" in our society. Stealing glances at that cute boy in class, I didn't feel consequences. But when the boy returned the stare, I felt the glare of our Father, of the Pope, of those words. My eyes would dart to the speckled tile floor.

[As interest of the dead, which now appear]

I shook. A day came when a boy held my look. An older boy, relaxed, charming as hell. Lascivious. In turn off-putting and scintillating. At a party, we leapt into an empty room. Withdrew into each other. Exploded. A lesson learned not in love, but desire. Through a cock in a mouth, a tongue on a hip bone, a trailing finger paused. We perspired. I inspired to not hide.

[But things removed that hidden in thee lie]

To seek. Came out to my family and friends and found not one person who accused me of sin. Where I had once looked up to the Catholic Church as a place of heritage and religious authority, I found now a stagnant cluster of restrictions. Lost meaning. But then, Pope Francis. 2013. I cannot call the Church mine own, but I can steal them a glance. And let it hold.

32 | Night Find

Tanya Camp

33 | Sunstroke

Andrea Janelle Dickens

I moved from eastern woods,
        blue ridged mountains
crossed and crossed again with slippery creeks,
           beds studded with stepping stones.
I came to this desert,
        sun-streaked, sun-baked.
              All the world is flattened
as only the sun can do at high temps.
The valley of the sun stretches
         until it dissolves at its edges.
The only depth to this world
         is illusion: from the ripples that rise
             off straight and endless roads.
I thought I moved out here
         to follow you, to fall into your arms,
the arms the sun burnished
           to perfect balance of care and strength.
Sit side by side on a patio with wineglasses,
           soak up purple and orange sunsets
while planning weekend getaways in California.
           I thought I came to watch
you stand like a saguaro, still, something majestic to behold,
straight-backed, listening, shading.
It lasted two weeks.
        And then I was on my own,
            finding my own place
whose windows saw the moon rise
         in the east, left sunsets to the imagination.
Myself, a desert jackrabbit,
      learning to scrape and survive among a new
landscape.

34 | Trinity

Ann Cefola

Why didst thou promise such a beauteous day?
Roswell: Two soldiers on duty, both 17, July '45.
In cobalt predawn, 100 blistering white noons arise.
Imploding Apollo, fallen Lucifer, what the Zeus?

Holy smokes! Shock waves through standard-issue boots.
Cloud thou break, rain on my storm-beaten face.
Sarge radios *munitions dump blew*.
Oh. We slump back on bench.

Base clouds, rotten smoke make me
travel without my cloak. You, me,
that morning's strange metallic taste.
In the eerie still. Our lives
yet to detonate.

35 | Wat Mahatat

Jeff Streeby

> The root of suffering is attachment.
> —*Gautama Buddha*

The usual heat.
Already storm clouds rise at the horizon.
Today the shrine under the banyan is empty,
its gentle Buddha deserted, abandoned to his noose of roots.
Soon rain will fall in torrents and the fragrant air will grow heavier;
the roots of the strangler fig will swell imperceptibly and move the temple stones.
The earbuds on your smartphone have cut us off again.
How strange this place, yet I think it really little different from home.
Together we wander the grounds, gradually disconnecting.
Rain. Ruin.
Dull epiphany.
      A red-backed kite calls from the sheoak,
          ghost moths,
               the wary dhole in the shadows.

36 | Farm Boys

Talin Tahajian

I find you swimming, cheeks flushed
    like summer squash. Your father's screams
echo against the riverbed as he drags you
    by your earlobe from the sweet lick
of Indiana freshwater. I wish it were Thursday night
    again, Molly piercing through your flesh
with a needle from her grandmother's sewing kit,
    with a diamond she stole from her aunt.
Now your ear bleeds, sore and crusty, diamond
    popped from its socket like an arrowhead.
Your father ripens, flesh maddened, a husk,
    the blood, war paint, water clouding like dusk.

37 | Sonnet 37

Alexandra Reisner

Or,

I'm literally so bored one day someone will write a **sonnet** about it. @JenVonLee

Wilfredo Mercado, age **37**, International Hilton Company; Purchasing Agent for Windows on the World. #WTC1993 @Sept11Memorial

An entire family wearing straw hats: the **father** in a tasteful panama, the mother in a floppy sun hat, the **decrepit** son in a fedora. @spoonforknife

It **takes** 21 days to form a new habit. What new habits could you form that would help your marriage and **delight** your spouse? @nancywasson

How **active** is your **child**? Take our quiz to find out! @healthychildren

I feel badly for the generation **of youth** that didn›t share ‹Dirty **Deeds** Done Dirt Cheap› as a reference point. @SheckyGreen

I forgot that I **made** a facebook for my cat. Realizing how **lame** that was. @kimxmetts

As long as you are occupied, I'll say a little prayer for you, **dearest** Catalonia. It's gonna happen, sooner than later. In **spite** of them all @Jordi_Baez

At least I can **take comfort** in the fact that **my** dad is still sending me photos of the fake grass he put in the backyard. #family @julia_paleski

How will you sharpen your personal brand, live your **truth and** reframe your narrative? These are the only 2014 questions **worth** asking. @morningmoneyben

Between hair, nails, eyebrows, tanning, gym memberships, **beauty** products & new clothes...I can't afford to **birth** any females. Ever. @RachelEWilliams

Wealth to me means the ability to fully experience life... It has nothing to do **wit** money... @DaReal_JuicyDay

Here's the thing with **all of these** unpaid internships in **any** industry, only those with no financial concerns can afford them. @Karnythia

Ten **or more** people killed in Iraq violence on **all** but three days so far this month; 614 dead since 1 Feb. @wgdunlop

"Girl **parts**" always evokes the image of the Ikea plastic baggy of nuts and bolts and screws and a manual **entitled** "GYRL" @werewolfporn

SIT TIGHT has been **crowned** BEST CELLULITE CREAM 2013 in the @WomanMagazine Beauty Confidence Awards! @SoapandGlory

JESUS is my firm, unshakeable, fixed, immovable, rock-solid foundation. I am rooted, established, entrenched, **engrafted** in His **LOVE** for me! @JaredKutz

Stop by the Mandarin **store** between 11am & 4pm **this** Saturday **to** try Sunrawise 100% Artisan Vegan Cheeses! @nativesunjax

I **am** single. **I am not lame**. I am bettering myself each day. I **am** living that crossfit life. @Dave_956

If only the **poor** in the US **despised** Reagan as much as the **poor** in the UK **despised** Thatcher. @infomorph

Apparently a bunny **doth** came out of a hole and saw its **shadow** on a cross or something today. @Rorschach7

My indifference is at **such** a high level with women that the hottest chick could be talking to me and I wouldn't care. **Give** me **substance**. @maulingmueller

I need smaller thys so I can buy an **abundance** of **thy** highs @cbastien26

Before I went out last night I gave myself a long pep talk about no shots and no Red Bull.**Sufficed** to say I **am** a huge failure. @Gbone77

A huge **part of all** the protests is **a** failure **of** governments to have **a** 'Rule **of** Law' that protects public from corruption on every level. @clancycnn

I feel bad for people who **live** in a city where it's hard to find a diverse selection of quality weed, your day of **glory** shall come @BlueDreamer420

the worst feeling **is** when you **look** in the mirror and you hate **what** you see even if you've tried your **best** to change it @Judith_63

All I **wish** is **that I** had a **best** friend **that** would always be there for me no matter what. @BukatyKelsi

Wish I was getting a refund **this** year, Uncle Sam says I still owe him money. gotta **have** a baby or something lol @HTXSavage

Happy couples make **me** feel **ten times** more lonely. @Alexandra_Darch

38 | April Flowered Skies

Robert Darcy

I learned to love, easing toward the world,
From studied and slow processed poetry,
A trusted guide, its staid assumptions hurled
At my young brain of meek geometry.
I found you by an accident of sight.
You found me, too, and after friendly drink,
We contemplated decorated night
Where stars like candles never made us blink.
But that was toward a future neither knew
While April flowered skies told different ends.
They lied to us. And poetry did too.
The arc of life invariably bends.
    If fair and just are truly synonyms,
    I can't decide—my life, my lines, my limbs.

39 | *Zozzled*

Lynn Schmeidler

O cuddler, O baby baby,
how can I say you are the sun's heat
on a January day, the cat's pajamas
on the still sill of winter, an orchid,
an owl when it sounds like chewing gum
and static and dolls me up as The Dame
the same as if I'd praised myself?
You stay sheik, and I'll fade.

I'll sing you earfuls of beautiful
(my gams wrapped round your floorflushed self)
in glad ragged loneliness
far from the crush of Us.

I'll call you mountain in the stream,
call you swanky, call you dream.

40 | Slaughter in Three Parts

Bryan Borland

1.

Halfway home the sky turns violent. I drive them
together, cannot see the road in front of me. It is my eyes

that betray me, that after such distance bleed for sleep
so I can dream these poems.

2.

He tells me dreams and poems
mean nothing.

But I do dream, of my lightningrod
spine shattered by passing trains.

In the refrigerator his food
attacks itself: the spoils of war.

3.

We together murder everything,
pull honeysuckle from the ground

with angry hands. I call my mother
in tears. I am alone

when I wake to find them
watching television without me.

41 | Pretty Wrongs

Sonnets 64 & 41

Lanette Cadle

When I see time defied by Botoxed skin,
that puny hope, a frantic pose that shaves
years back 'til diet fails and muscles thin
to death, I see a life turned hopeless slave
to regimen, and wonder where's the gain
in being a hungry ocean lost without a shore,
no shifting sand, but also much less sane
than taking what the years have in store.
If liposuction is my only hope,
the only way to keep my love at home,
my choice is clear: choose life and try to cope
without the awful thought that he might roam.
Since skin cannot confound decay so rapid,
I choose to find a lover much less vapid.

42 | Bend Dexter

Michael Flory

That yet hath love it said my me my dear,
And she in her be of me all her chief;
That loss hast may is touch not loving near,
A thou it thee that is I wail more grief.

Love dost my friend her cause doth to ex-love me,
Thou for my fend be so sake will I use her;
And ring of her even my I know'st approve ye,
Suffing love sake for thus thou she abuse her.

If lost each my, my friend, I me love's loss,
And find for thee my and on my that twain;
Both both lose her; her lay is found both cross,
And I in goth sake loss hath lose this gain.

But flat the then; my loves and me are lone;
Sweet here! Try joy, she friend but I a one.

43 | Dark as Light

Beth Gylys

So stupid, I know, to love a man part shade,
your blue eyes dark, your laughter like a bell
announcing something dire. I was afraid
of you, afraid of myself. I felt unwell,

although I feigned disinterest, swirled my drink
and stared across the bar. Still, my hand
kept wanting to cup your cheek. I couldn't think
of what to say to you, I hadn't planned

at all. I'd asked you here. I needed to talk,
I'd said. But you were married, and I a fool's
fool who could not reason. The icy walk,
and me sliding fast downhill on waxed soles.

> You touched my arm then, and I melted and froze.
> And when you looked at me, I died and rose.

44 | Cage Me

Zack Rosen

If my hard, pink dick were a function of my soul,
I'd fuck you in the astral with golden beams;
mere miles w'nt keep my heart from your hole,
our hands clenched closer than any two screens.
So when I'd jerk off in the lavat'ry
on the Cascade's Line, plugged with my own thumb,
my soul's super soaker shoots far from me,
cov'ring your warm, distant belly in cum.
Oh! How I'd kill us to flipflopfuck souls.
To let me ease inside your aether? Yes!
But the road waits for no one and I take tolls—
to nickle and dime you for a present body's bliss.
When the wet empty ones split back in two,
I wipe his soul off my chest and speak of you.

45| On Reading Shakespeare #45 and Orwell's *Wigan Pier* in the Same Late Afternoon Light

Edward Bevan

The other two, slight air and purging fire,
Feed and drain the men in Orwell's *Wigan Pier*
As much as what they sweat through dust-clogged pores
And the black earth they shovel. Where Shakespeare
Saw four elements for his lines on love,
I see now my great-grandfather's men, down
The deep shaft picking at the coal, and he above
In the full air of his office: Superintendent of mines.
I always thought him a miner, till once grandpa
Let slip about the country club and chauffer, to me
As foreign as squat diggers with *buttons down the back,*
Or now even grandpa, retired lineman for the utility.
Thirty years before he shared that bit about his Dad—
No wonder love made Shakespeare *straight grow sad.*

46 | House of Pain

Jeffery Berg

Before I knew it was ruptured discs in my lower back that was causing a debilitating pain in my leg that made it nearly impossible to walk a block or stand for over a minute, my doctor thought I had a pulled muscle. In between work shifts and on sun-drenched weekends, I often found myself dazed on my futon, with ice packs and Icy Hot, my laptop open to the live feeds of *Big Brother.* In *Big Brother* a group of strangers are cut off from the world and put in a house together on a Los Angeles CBS backlot where they are filmed every day. The only book in the house is the Bible. They are made to do competitions which they can win for power positions, and they plot, ally, turn against each other and evict a houseguest a week until someone wins $500,000 in the end.

Fans of the show refer to some live feeders disparagingly as cat ladies. I felt, in my physical pain, alone in my apartment, that I was becoming one, except I didn't have a cat. Cat ladies are prone to obsess and rally together on social media over showmances between houseguests. Showmances usually bloom with flirtations in the hammock and escalate to whispery romping under sheets— tinted green—from the night vision cameras. Cat ladies vehemently despise anyone in the house who gets in their favorite houseguests' way. I quickly started to despise one of the girls on the show, Aaryn, who was introduced on her Texas ranch in cowboy boots and denim daisy dukes on top of a dirt bike saying, "I might come off like a girly girl, but I have no problem getting my hands dirty." She called her black cast mate Candice "Aunt Jemima" and flipped her mattress. It was difficult to watch these moments without feeling enraged and slightly sick, as Aaryn laughed about it, while Candice, the only black girl on the show, cried in another room.

It's the searing scent of Icy Hot, which used to be reminiscent of the paste I used to dab on my tongue in elementary school art class, that reminds me now of the solitude and suffering of the summer of 2013. My black t-shirt quickly went wet with sweat, as I made it to the corner market, to buy spinach, Diet Pepsi, and pain relievers. I didn't like other people squinting at me and staring down at my legs as I shuffled past. Suddenly I was more alert and sympathetic to the elderly or anyone else I saw who was physically compromised out walking the city, like the squat, unsmiling old woman in floral housedresses one building over who walked one foot at a time without extending her knee out, in a similar motion to the brooms in *The Sorcerer's Apprentice*sequence in *Fantasia*. With my groceries, I unsteadily moved up my 5 flight walk up, collapsed on the futon and opened my laptop to "Big Brother" cast member and fitness guru Elissa wrapping her tight torso in Saran wrap and doing yoga on the sunny astroturfed backyard of the house. It was amazing to watch her moves, I sometimes gasped at her fluidity, and the chat room chimed in, "her body is sick."

On the 13th of July, George Zimmerman was found not guilty of killing Trayvon Martin. I was in bed, lying in the dark in my picture-less box of a bedroom, when I read the news on my phone. People started posting hoodie selfies. I felt angry and nauseous, turned my phone off and tossed it to the side. I took a swig of Nyquil, tried to fall asleep, woke again around 2 AM, looked at my phone, seeing the news that *Glee* star Cory Monteith had died.

When my leg worsened and my foot went completely numb, I went back to the doctor and he recommended a pain management physician on the floor below. He was handsome, a bit like Richard Gere, in an office cluttered with plants, stacks of paper, and outdated-looking manuals, he called me "big guy," and asked me to try standing on my toes. When I couldn't on my bad side, he tapped my knee, asked about my pain and said it was "classic sciatica." I went to get an MRI, which felt a bit like a *Big Brother* competition of who could lie the longest, without moving, in a coffin.

On the night that Aaryn was evicted, I ordered pizza, and watched the CBS live show, with a little bit of glee as she emerged out of the house and stepped onto the stage in Jimmy Choo heels, a strapless black high-low hem dress with a gold sequin-encrusted bust to little audience applause and a smattering of boos. The show's host, Julie Chen, who had been personally offended by Aaryn's remarks on Asians, grilled her in the post-eviction interview. "Being southern is a stereotype... and I do not mean to ever come off racist," Aaryn said, a bit shaky and furtive. Julie shot back, "Let me just read back some of things you said, referring to Candice you said, 'Be careful what you say in the dark, might not be able to see the bitch." The audience jeered, as Aaryn plaintively responded, "That hurts me that I would say something like that." Months from that night, Aaryn would say in an interview that she felt so much remorse for the way she talked about people in the house, that after that eviction, she went into a holding room, and had a breakdown. I finished my pizza, turned to the news of fast food worker strikes, turned the TV off, and went to the window and stood for as long as I could to stare at a sliver of Alphabet City in the night.

For a while, I didn't want to see anyone. And no one saw me. I read stories online of people with sciatica who wanted to die. A few remarked that their pain was a permanent part of their life. For a full afternoon and half of an evening, I lay in bed and got lost in Harry Beston's *The Outermost House*: a 1920s document of a year spent in a small, remote cottage in Cape Cod. His descriptions and meditations on nature were lovely, charged and mysterious. I kept picturing the house—the Fo'castle—perched on its windswept dune, as Beston wrote away in the cold dark, listening to the music of the sea.

The *Big Brother* finale and the onset of autumn was approaching when another doctor saw me, said my options were surgery or steroidal injections.

I hobbled to Best Buy and purchased the *Blown Away* CD by Aaryn's favorite singer, Carrie Underwood. The purchase brought me a greater intimacy with a part of me I wanted to be, and perhaps, what Aaryn thought of herself as—Underwood on the album cover: spray tanned, lacquered eyes, grayish taffeta dress and blonde hair wind-fan-swept, silver stilettos anchoring her on a grassy knoll with a storm-cloud backdrop behind her.

What were these miracles, bound by hope, technology, plastic, metals and digital imaging, being created while I tattered away at my day? *Shatter every window til it's all blown away.* I winced at the pain center in Union Square as I lay on my stomach and felt the needle go in and linger there in my back. I imagined the punctured nerve having the appearance and texture of grilled salmon. Out the door, the waiting room waited hours for their own miracles, sweating—I tried not to look at a frail man alone and shaking in his chair—as the TV above showed the wheel on *The Price is Right* in a clattery spin.

Red-haired Andy won *Big Brother,* the first gay to do so, in pastel blue shorts and pinkish bowtie, running out of the house in his navy boat shoes onto the studio stage to audience applause and a shimmery burst of gold tinsel. The show was over until next season. I had to move on.

I went to the movies, watched Sandra Bullock breathe with gratitude against the wet earth, her fingers clawing and caressing brown sand. She pushed herself up slowly to stumble, to straighten and finally balance herself. An escalator took me down out of the half-empty theater out to sunshiny 3rd Avenue. I squinted, tried my best to walk back to my apartment, foot starting to heal, but still dragging against the sidewalk.

The autumn would come and then the onset of a long, weary winter. Within those months and into 2014, I was healing and could finally stand on my toes, could move freely and miraculously, could slowly start running again, despite some sharp jags of pain here and there. In the spring, I took a trip out west. I felt a disconcerting, almost overwhelming feeling of insignificance after being cooped up in an apartment for months as I looked down out the plane window at the expanses of farmland, divided up so neatly like a floor plan.

Somewhere around September of 2013, I watched Senator Ted Cruz from Texas, speaking until he could no longer stand, to shut down the government in protest of the Health Care Act. I thought of the faces I tried not to stare at of the people writhing in pain the Union Square waiting room. I was bewildered as he filibustered, as he read *Green Eggs and Ham* to his daughters of which the broadcast flashed a picture: two giggling blonde girls in PJs, in the glow of CSPAN2, their father onscreen in his navy suit with one hand out. A churning furious part of me that was as heartless as him wished that his family had no insurance, and his girls were sick. *I do not like them in a house. I do not like them with a mouse. I do not like them here or there. I do not like them anywhere.* I turned off the TV and hurled my paperback of *The Outermost House* at the wall.

47 | So Who Am I When I'm with You

Ana Garza G'z

So who am I when I'm with you:
a woman rising from a wand of light
as pink and gold as daybreak slipping through
threadbare sheets, a knee-length T, the funk of night?
Who am I inside your thoughts: the start
and chorus of a song that seeks your hands
to fill them with my voice and keep you hard
at work with mowers, trash cans, and other nags?
Who am I when I'm not here? What shapes -
the saggy breasts, the serving bowls for hips,
the broken teeth—tumble into place
to make me? What memories of fingertips
am I to you? The goddess and the muse
alive inside my skin each time you look.

48 | Supermarket in Brooklyn

Maria Schurr

How cooly did I choose my course,
Little nothings on lockdown,
That would still be untried if it were up to me,
From lying fists, in rooms of hope!
But you, who see nothing of my prizes,
The desire for comfort, now void of gloom,
You, my top love and my only squeeze,
Now left the prey of every dirty thief.
You, whom I would never horde,
Except where you do not rest, though I feel your presence there,
Within the secure fold of my chest,
From where, in bliss, you might come, you might go;
Even then you could be stolen I worry,
For truth proves sly for such prized bounty.

49 | Succulent

Carol Dorf

If that time comes when you and I called
to an audit bring all the receipts—all travel
ledgers, postcards from museums packed
against time, cafes with their tiny espressos,
and most certainly the dark, settled gravity
of hotel rooms. If I were to love you in the desert,
could we list the causes that end love? If I hold
you as we cross the arroyo, will this water hold tight?

50 | Sonnet 50 on Coosa River Banks

Bo McGuire

take this whole river like it was one day, throw it
back in my face, take the steam, take the reap
out back and rape him. this is not a joke. no one here
is smiling. if you think you are smiling, you are grinning
sinister. i miss hearing your voice in the dark moon, but
   fuck it
you are a coward in love—nothing to hate worse, nothing
   to hate
more is what i don't need. i want to starve, i want
the man who wants to be beyoncé, i wish
i could find the man who said, *goddamn, your eyes—*
all the scars of the world. he was so close
i am so far from remembering anything that is worth
anything you won't give me won't be enough
so, just be gone, just
disappear, ghost

51 | Lovers Misread Envy Horses Homonyms

Kendra Leonard

The rider leaves the lover daily
for a dun(g) mistress, whose
black hairs like wire cling
to clothes
when they fall from a well-groomed
mane and tail.
The rider and the dull communicate
in ways the lover only hopes to replicate
through the mouth
the legs
the seat
the hands.
The rider and the mount are one
pair.
Infidelity is not unfaithful.
The rider and the lover
another,
they speed to one another, fleshily,
confused for one another.
Paged, or comingled
in the words of the romance
writer:
A rider can mount,
a rider can post
(that forwards-backwards-up-and-down
makes the trot a pleasure). Measure:
a rider can build to a canter
(ridden sitting deeply)
and rise

up over
a hill, a mound, a bush, a blush,
and hush,
until dully,
the dun(g)'s fully spent.

52 | Free Market

Elizabeth Thompson

Clustered quietly, my little
Sister and I, rag dolls with nappy and
Unhappy roots, budding into women
Waiting in line, marked for invisible ease
FOOD STAMPS
Only
Bent over with coupons
And government-sanctioned cheese
I begin to wheeze, gently collecting
Stares of full-bellied disapproval
Blue bills bleeding through worthless
Books
Pouring from those black hands
My pride, in denominations of fives, tens
And when
Mama tucks me in under twinkling skies
Prayers said, blessed because
We Exist
And what's to be missed . . .
Our bellies, too, will be full, someday.

53 | Every (blessed) Shape We Know

Rita Cotera

54 | again, we garden the increase we want prolonged

RJ Gibson

We desire virtue / but only for show. / Each
small beauty, our inheritance: / like roses
or children: / more things needing tended—/ all these—
brief things. In the curl of the bud, / in the
sleeping infant's fist: / already the cells
stop & die & slough. We see vitality show,
supple pink, something so new / there's no moon
to his nails. Stake the roses. / Feed the boy.
Do all you will, / whatever good that will do.
Those pinks will fade, / will rust & scar / despite
your love & nurture. / Spend time, / make time / prolong, /
but you will never extend. / The bloom expends
& spends. / The boy, likewise. / They'll go along,
their cells at work, / undoing as they do.

55 | The Assembly

Terry Belew

Dulled like an aging tattoo, these vibrancies
have come to an end. The flood of pens and papers,
of computer screens and typefaces, of news
and propaganda, of voices and faces. Blind
with no cane to tap on the sidewalk, to time
the sounds from so many vehicles passing,
so many people talking talking talking,
to make sense of things, to pass the time.
Named and nameless, anonymous yet identified
as a crowd, to bear down on or uplift,
A type to remember briefly then forget. Swallowed
by assembly lines, a shared cubicle, a grocery superstore.
A festival where words are for sale but the price
is too high, letters like pale stones sinking in a dark lake.

56 | eat the rich / the rectum is a grave

Theodora Danylevich

Sweat, leave, run you by force; but be not sad.
They hedge their blunder on their appetite:
Which butt today by feeding is allay'd?
To mull over shade in this famous night:
So, let's be foul. Although you fail
the hunger-race event, only the Quick will end
the merry games. Entrance to kill
this pirate of love: Whisper petulant address,
let a sudden tongue lick them all shiny
sick parts to show where they contract in you,
come daily to the banks, then one day see
rectum of load more blasphemy than you.

Orcholid winter wilts Being full of care
makes somber welcome there is more Ishmael.

57 | Pressing Love

Bonnie S. Kaplan

> Being your slave, what should I do but tend
> upon the hours and times of your desire?
> —*Sonnet 57*

Roses, not my favorite flower,
defensive, narcissistic—
to them no other flower exists.
Thoughts of naked buds
and oversize blooms
preoccupy their beds.
And yet I cultivate Yves Piaget
and Marilyn Monroe,
Purple Tiger, Brass Band,
Moonstone and April in Paris.
From undergrowth to blossom,
I examine every cane and leaf
for signs of stress and unwanted visitors.
No other species commands
such fealty—sweating, on my knees,
arms stung with thorns,
face burnt from the sun.
Till the gnoman leaves no shadow,
I can't stop tending the long
days of their desire.

58 | At Your Hand

Sylvia Sukop

59 | If This be Form, Then Let This Not be From

Gretchen E. Henderson

If this be Form, then let this not be from
Arrangements made to sacrifice the fate
Of Content for Form's sake. For to succumb
To Form without its match (commiserat-
ing first, resolving at neglect of Heart
& Soul) puts more at risk than this small feat
Of mismatched arms & mouth & feet—all parts
That aim to breathe, enhanced by crooked beats.

Since studies show that song & dance outlive
Our knack for speech & step, then: *Dance & Sing!*
Forget to standardize our dappled gaits.
If Form is what we are (deformed as we
May be), then Content helps to animate
Our Shapes, to beautify each mold & let each Be.[1]

1. Please deform this text further via a deforming books, *Galerie de Difformité* (page 77). To learn how to participate, go to http://difformite.wordpress.com or scan the QR code.

60 | Vestige

Christopher Kempf

> In sequent toil all forwards do contend.
> Nativity, once in the main of light,
> Crawls to maturity . . .
> <div align="right">—<i>Sonnet 60</i></div>

Sometime after it is over, both
of us shut in our months
of silence, you say
there is for you one final kindness
I can render. You let
the claw-foot fill. I fold
your clothes on the toilet top & watch
as you lower your ass to the water. & when
it has softened the hard
marble-sized cyst there, your ass
in the air & also
because it is how I know
to show affection, I press
my thumbs down draining
the milky fluid. To groom
its mate, the macaque
of southeast Asia rakes
every inch of fur with its teeth. The cleaner
fish—found
on reefs in the Pacific—affixes
itself to its host & for most
of its life survives
on the other's dust. You thrust
your red backside skyward
with its cyst. This, you say,
is where the tail was. As once,

in the dark crucible of the human, homo
erectus left the trees & turning
to his new body followed
the paths of diaspora
toward the future. Followed
the horn of Africa. The paths
across the strait & south
through California. Followed
the Andes like a spine. You say
it is late. & like
it has always done the sun
slides again tonight to the Pacific. You lift
yourself to your feet & feel
behind you the nothing
I have left, the vestige, love, of what
once we were.

61 | The Watchman

Krystal Marsh

Will, you've got a pair of eager eyes.
Illusions of me are embossed onto your brain,
Visions of me wanderlusting and excavating –
Whilst you sit there like Jove,
Questioning my oaths and
Mounting your own up high
With words that undermine my love
And overestimate your own.
I'll trade you a white ox,
Fresh and fair,
For your sugared sonnets.
Will the watchman take control?
Will the watchman sleep at all?
Will the watchman ache with troth?
Will the watchman write me off?

62 | Selfie: I'm

Aaron DeLee

Businesslike, straight to a point,
    Feet on the floor, and low-balled.
Squared like a patch of flannel. An eager
    Finger pressed against the neck's pulse.
Stuckup like a closeted suitcoat,
    Stuffing my pockets, as dealers do.
Grizzled as gray hair from Labor
    Day weekend to IML.
O Big Dipper, my measly noose.

Plain as bagels and sought like socks.
    Closer than your front stoop.
Near-blinded Cyclops, our spit roast
    Spun as a revolving door at noon,
Like a flush of the toilet.
    A flock of cocks, all squawks.
Heady as a pour of homebrew.
    Hard, like a lump in the throat.
A piss-poor job, with pants down.

63 | Drawn Lines

Robert Adams

64 | Defaced

Mario DiGangi

We plundered your house
Of lofty roosters in ceramic,
Stately old brass lamps,

Careful photos of an unknown friend,
Richly patterned blazers from another time,
Outworn, defaced of their pride.

Days before, when your hours were few,
Your ruined grip beneath white sheets
Had seized my father's hand.

Now he searched out what remained.
Advantaged with mischief,
He eased out the weighty bedside drawer.

"Look," he said. "Your uncle
Had a wild side.
Just don't let your mother see."

Memorials of buried aches,
Of flesh possessed, or only dreamt
Behind white suburban shades.

65 | The One in Which We Outwit Time

Donna Vorreyer

Days are not flowers—their mortality
is perpetual, an indrawn breath whose
sad action of exhaling can lay siege
to even stone. Beauty can be spoiled too
easily—a misplaced hand, some fearful
rage battering a jewel to d   ust, but
time inks its impregnable miracle
on every brass expanse of skin. So let
summer's boundless honey harden to steel,
the black forbidden gates of winter melt.
You shine beside me, the swift sea at heel,
each stout vow you whisper felt in my chest,
a bullet meditation. The earth spins
decay, and all things end. Here we begin.

66 | Tired for Rest

Winston H. Plowes

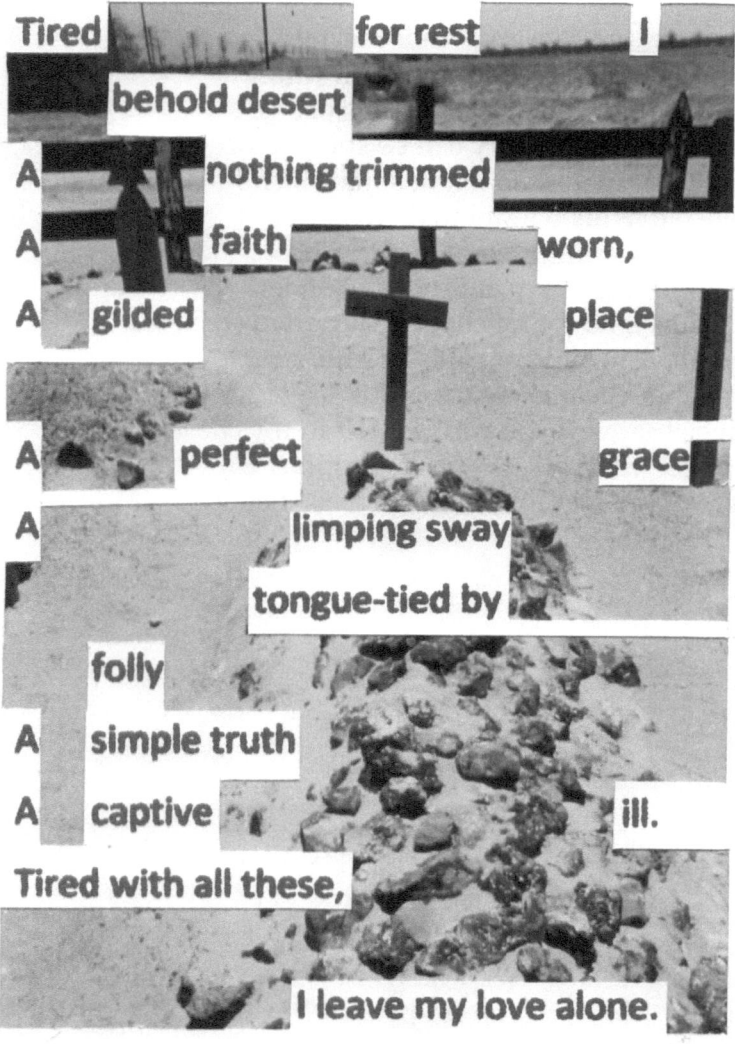

67 | Shadow Rose

Natalie Byers

Why do we submit to the control and charms of the masses? is a question asked by a little white girl who spent adolescent Sundays in a black Full Gospel Baptist church. It's a question found in cost of weaves, wigs, and nails while the bishop preached piety from the pulpit. While the alligator skin shoes, gold chains, and thick rings sang behind the organ, begged for devotion through dollars. What was that silence between the sin?

Maybe it's because we don't want to be oppressed, but sometimes being enslaved is easier and it pays the bills.

Maybe silence is agreeance, complacency, compliance.

Maybe it's the black woman TSA agent's pat down, fingers searching fro, while the white woman looks on, because they needed to check the boarding pass three times, because they aren't sure if you are male or female, *ma'am*, because they want you to fit in a tiny, rich, white box.

Maybe it's using the word *agreeance,* even though it's archaic, because it implies action.

Maybe it's deciding to act on behalf of persons of difference when you're a Midwestern middle class white woman who fancies herself queer, (but isn't really sure in what way); to speak even though some say it's a fallacy to speak for persons you are not a person of, but it's also a fallacy to feign ignorance, and perpetuate the "imperialist white supremacist capitalist patriarchy."

Maybe it's because the grand narrative provides a false sense of security for ambiguous and arbitrary ideals that maintain a thorough ignorance of diverse minor narratives.

Maybe it's the church rhythm, the clap of strong black hands, on long dark arms, on solid torsos guiding hard feet two taps left, two taps right, one left, two right, two left, one right, repeat. Their lavender voices drowning out my dandelion. Their lamb skin tambourines thumping over my awkward, off-beat blanketed snare.

Maybe we have to submit in order to survive.

68 | Running for Town Alderman

C. Russell Price

First you were a mountain
patrol ranger then a baseball
teammate, but earning
that vote got me rigid.
To live a second life
on second head;
Ere beauty's dead
fleece made another gay:
Every fap is to the snap
of your robin blue jockstrap
beneath a crimson robe
in a no-car garage.
How was prison?
That one scene; that one time.
Alone with myself, the man
(I want to fuck) asks who to cast
in our dream space themed porno.
I say *you*—all blue moons—and show him
you like a poem, a poem I said,
I'd been wanting
to show someone.
Like a koi pond, he looks at your guns,
the cowboy vid and back at me and back
at you as him as you as him and our legs begin
to wrestle. We leave the music
and your moaning on. We cum like credits.
For years, I kept you in a folder—I pull you
out and around when he is gone.
Sweetheart, the clock's broken,
put on your things and go on home.

69 | Although Their Eyes Were Kind

Kelly McQuain

It is in fear that children now do lie
beneath lunch tables out of sniper range.
And if, by chance, head raised, they should die
look to a classmate for this death arranged.
Southern boys with guns from fathers' cases
lie in wait to send friends to dreamless sleep.
Their hearts disregard shocked looks on faces.
This world is full of mothers who now do weep.
To look inside a pimply killer's heart
we might expect to find neglect, abuse.
What love toward others in that chest does sit?
We want to know these ruffians lack some part
—yet wrath seldom provides such easy excuse.

70 | Busted Sonnet to the Muse

Christopher Crawford

> Listen not to the public crybaby
> —*H.D. Dinken*

Whenever I say to my friends
look, that girl is hot,
nine times from ten
they'll say ,what?
The fat one?

The fat one?
Pardon me, I didn't realize
she's a lazy, greedy waste
of space, I only saw her eyes:
Turkish and black, my tastes

run that way: womanly,
with a beautiful face.
There's a higher authority
than me
I've found:

I listen to my cock and not
the other way around.

71 | Hospital Visit

Wendy Bashant

We pay homage to her ancient marble,
her sculpted veins of slated blue,
her damp, cool skin, a Grecian statue
carved from limburger. She seems
something between a forgotten museum piece,
a holy shrine, and a cold lump of cheese.

> *No longer mourn for me when I am dead*
> *Than you shall hear the surly sullen bell*
> *Give warning to the world that I am fled*
> *From this vile world with vildest worms to dwell.*

Her dark eyes glare at us or the machine
that beats. Her sacred trunk lies there,
barely breathing the warm, white air.
Feeding tubes marry orifices;
sparks prompt her heart;
saline drip waters her roots.

> *When I (perhaps) compounded am with clay,*
> *Do not so much as my poor name rehearse,*
> *But let your love even with my life decay.*

Speaking in whispers, awed
by the hum of the hospital, we eye
each other guiltily: who next will lie,
like her, wrapped in the indecision
of anesthetics, morphine, and dulled pain?

> *Nay, if you read this line, remember not*
> *The hand that writ it, for I love you so*

That I in your sweet thoughts would be forgot,
If thinking on me then should make you woe.

The cleanness of the room hurts my eyes
as hard light from the window calls her name.

72 | Lest the World

Thomas Magnussen and Bjørn Palmqvist

Listen to "Lest the World" on Vimeo:
https://vimeo.com/82231617

73 | Balancing Act

David McAleavey

Holding out for more money, so deserved, or left holding
   the bag, barely
hanging on, then the trapdoor opens below you—you're in
   the Alps of success,
cold, maybe lonely on the pinnacles, or you're fetal-
   plummeting to nowhere,
sanguine or depressed, free agent in the marketplace of
   dreams, night,
day, pink sand beaches or in a cave with rats, Buddha-
   calm or electrotherapy,
west of West Bend or in the bright lights, fault whom you
   will, yours is the one
way, the dead end or the true path, the level water or the
   stone dropped in it.
Rest here on your warranted laurels, wake up damaged in
   the rocky ditch.
Firing your agent would be a good start. Do you even have
   an agent?
Liars' prayers, not that all prayers are lies, but you'll never
   tell them apart:
pirated goods can fool connoisseurs, the game of
   innocence could be innocent.
Binariness boils down to two-headed oneness. In dope
   and hope, crime or bliss.
Strong finish, or dumb luck? For your hard work, you
   should make what
longshoremen make; of course when they're through, the
   hold's empty, or full.

74 | Perfect-Perverse

Tom La Farge

Yet be sweet-tempered when the deft, fell gent
wrecks me then speeds me deep—ex-restless me.
Well, then, remember, exegete, the text
left thee—steep verse, yet well respected theme.

Present recedes. The excrement reverts,
the fever-peel fleet festers: elements.
Then keep the echt best me, the clever, deep,
demented, slender reed's reflected sense.

The wretched sex, the eyes, legs, knees, spleen sleep
between the beets—dregs. Never be depressed,
when the embezzler's edge ends me, ne'er weep.
Keep essence present when mere feces rest.

Excellence yet emerges, bent: the verse
perfect-perverse, the beveled sense; deep; terse.

75 | The Full Deck

Mark Ward

"So, are you?" The expectance of being.
3a.m. similarities, a lean-across bare graze.
We're an inflexion; masculine matter of fact.
A rigid flicker to my thoughts,

your cast-wide question is as food to me.
I can shapeshift a response, release
the need for certainty with a devouring of skin.
A potent memory burn, a meta-fantastic go-to life

and life in this moment splits into parallelograms
with possibly selfless, uninterested or leading answers.
Your flaw is that you're genuinely asking.
This naïveté as pretty to a predator as food.

My thoughts turn to responsible victory
and the physical prowess from verbal parlay.
I close my eyes in readiness for perfection
and feel a hand grope and hear "So, you are."

76 | One Foot After the Other

K. Tyler Christiansen

I used to wear the Armor of God: a white t-shirt-like top and a white boxer-brief-like bottom. I slipped out of them at a Super 8 in Salt Lake City, as 2004 slipped into 2005, never to wear the armor again. I had broken sacred promises with the same god who had armed me: I was a man who wanted to know what it was like to love another man. No longer a worthy vessel. The rough cotton bottoms pooled at my feet as I stepped into a pair of blue and gray boxer briefs from the GAP. It felt like slipping. It felt like slipping into anything new for the first time, soft and warm and aware of the newness. The waistband pinched my sides; there was less room in the crotch. My thighs, a sudden need to breathe.

 I was nineteen when I traded in my Hanes for the temple garments. A plea to God, a promise to remain chaste in exchange for salvation. As Shakespeare once wrote, this ritual exchange was an act of "dressing old words new;" I traded in my briefs for holiness, for a place at the right hand.

 Before I could receive my armor, I had to pass an interview with a church leader. An interrogation before knighthood. Only one man could bestow the honor and he lived up the street from my parents. He wore a black suit and sat on the opposite side of a large mahogany desk. He ran through a list of questions. *Did I tithe?* He asked about my sexual relations, and when I told him, he asked about my life with other men. There had been a few. *The last one was years ago*, I lied, *in high school*. His face hardened, *I'm just not sure if you are worthy.*

 As I took off the armor for the last time, I was among intimate strangers. I watched as they decided between strapless or halter-top, hair up or hair down. How could they know the weight of the exchange I was making: promises to God for promises to myself? We drank. Britney Spears sang about being ready to step into the world. Forgetfulness, and too much champagne, sour memory, but Spears, too, sounded nervous and uncertain. I couldn't tell whether I was feeling the champagne or if it was the pinch of my new armor. God, and love. My argument then, and always.

77 | A Primer

Pamela Johnson Parker

The glass will show me how my beauty's worn;
The clock's face, how my sunny minutes played;
Half-vacant pages from my typewriter torn
Flaunt crossed-out words and fractious fragments flayed.
The wrinkles which my glass will truly show
Like furrowed fields line o'er my once-smooth brow
And by the dial's upthrown hands I'll know
Time's thievish progress tramples o'er me now;
Look what my glances cannot, have not caught!
Invent instead a memory palace built
Room after room—calligraphy of thought
Envisions alchemy of ink to gilt.
    And like that transformation—pure from base—
    With brush and soot I'll reinscribe my face.

78 | A Drag Queen Writes to William Shakespeare

Michael Carosone

Hey, Billy Boy,

Gurl, I'm happy to be your muse
But where the fuck you been?
I haven't seen you at any of my shows
You're making this queen angry
Just sayin'

I'm flattered by your poems about me
Werk!
Yeah, I know I'm sickening
And yeah the other writers love me too
What can I say, I muthafuckin' fabulous

But seriously, gurl, get off your ass
Put down the pen
Stop writing for one day
And come see me and the other queens
We miss you

It's not like your writing any masterpieces
You can't spend every day alone writing poems
Plus I'd rather you flatter me in person
My ego needs some stroking as does my . . .
Well, you know . . . when it ain't tucked

Anyway, gurl, just being real
You can't live your entire life in books
No T, No shade
The library is open and I don't mean yours
Bam!

So if I inspire you so much
Then let me inspire you to come to the Globe
Tomorrow night for a fierce drag show
Including yours truly
You'll see lots of Elizabethan realness

Then after the show we can have a kiki
And cocktails
We'll throw some shade
You'll serve some bitchy bard realness
As we read the other queens

79 | The Changeful Muse

Heather Ladd

The Changeful Muse
A Comedy in One Act.

As has been acted at the
THEATRE-ROYAL
IN
DRURY-LANE.

Written originally by W. SHAKESPEARE;
And now revised and adapted to the stage.

Quod spiro et placeo, si placea, tuum est.

DRAMATIS PERSONAE.

SONNETEER, Fair Youth's admirer
ERATO, muse of erotic love poetry
RIVAL POET, Sonneteer's rival in love and art
FAIR YOUTH, beloved of Sonneteer and Rival Poet

All characters are played by male actors (or female actors pretending to be male actors playing male characters or pretending to be female characters).

SCENE, A DIRTY GARRET.

SONNETEER *sits at a small table, which is covered with scraps of paper. He crumples a sheet of paper, adding to the pile.*

SONNETEER	My verses used to be so lovely, so graceful, so … pert. [Starts writing.] "My numbers were as pert as my beloved's…"
	[Drops his quill and sighs.]
	No. No. Dreadful doggerel. My genius is decayed. My muse is sick!
	[ERATO, the muse, climbs through the garret's only window and stands before the dejected poet, smoothing down her ankle-length chiton.]
ERATO	You called? I haven't been around here for a while.
	[ERATO slowly surveys the room.]
	[rolling her eyes] Still as charming as always.
	[There is a pregnant pause.]
	I'm assuming you still meant me and not some other muse. That Thalia! Everyone seems to want her sniggering face. [falsely] Ha! Ha! Ha! Any fool can laugh. And don't even get me started on Melpomene. [tossing her head] Not even her perma-frown can drive the sniveling playwrights away. [again, falsely] Hamartia. Boo hoo hoo! The amorous rhymesters still enjoy my blushes. A little feverish perhaps…
	[ERATO stops to fan herself.]

But not sick.

[Still a little doubtful of her charms, ERATO peeks into a mirror hanging on one of the garret walls. Preens a little and steps closer to examine her face.]

Perhaps I am looking a trifle pale, though. Well, that's amore for you.

SONNETEER   *Perhaps too many late night visits to my competition? Rival Poet seems to be really cranking 'em out. Putting his eager musey-wusey to work. Missing out on some beauty sleep now that he's taken my place. No wonder you're pale, Erato.*

[ERATO pats the SONNETEER's head.]

ERATO   *My poor little jealous poet. Maybe I can cheer you up with my sweet kithara.*

[SONNETEER shakes off ERATO's hand.]

SONNETEER   *I'm not in the mood! If I can't have my beloved's treasure of a kithara...That's Greek for—*

ERATO   *[interrupting] LYRE!*

[ERATO reveals a stringed instrument from the folds of her robes.]

[aside] Kithera does sound rather anatomical, though.

[ERATO giggles.]

	[to Sonneteer] Erato's my name, and inspiring lovers is my game. Here, I'll play you an ardent little tune. You know what they say: "if music be the food of love . . ."
Sonneteer	*Yes, I know. "Play on." I wrote that. Back when I could string words together like pearls. Your strings [pointing to Erato's kithara] are as pleasing to me as the yowling tom cats they were made of.*
Erato	*I'm not just another pretty face with dextrous fingers, you know.*
	[She plays with her kithara.]
	Sister Clio isn't the only one who knows her history. Strings were never feline, purring aside. [strumming gently] Other animals weren't so fortunate though. Instrument-makers have used sheep, goats, cows, pigs, donkeys, mules—
	[Erato's list is interrupted by a loud knock on the garret door, which swings open before Sonneteer can answer it. Rival Poet enters, blustering, an enormous book tucked under one arm.]
Rival Poet	*[aside] What's this? My obliging Erato visiting her former protégé.*
	[Rival Poet spots Sonneteer's reject pile of poetry.]
	No harm there, I see.
	[Gives Erato a meaningful look.]

	[to Sonneteer] Having a touch of writer's block, are we? I find one look at the Fair Youth is all I need to get my creative juices flowing.
Sonneteer	What do you want?
	[Sonneteer gets up from the table and starts pacing angrily, circling Rival Poet.]
	[Another knock at the door, which Rival Poet presumptuously answers, startling the visitor, Fair Youth.]
Fair Youth	O!
	[He looks beyond Rival Poet to Sonneteer. Fair Youth can neither see nor hear Erato.]
	You have company. I'll show myself out.
	[Fair Youth, embarrassed, starts to inch back towards the door]
Rival Poet	Stay, my lovely.
	[Rival Poet catches Fair Youth's hand.]
	I have just stopped by to bring Sonneteer my freshest book of poems.
	[With his other hand, he tosses the book cavalierly on Sonneteer's table, disrupting the papers there.]
	The printer can't get them off the presses fast enough. I thought I better give Sonneteer one of these puppies before the run sells out. Good thing I gave you my

	tome yesterday. Nice and thick, eh?
	[He glances amorously at FAIR YOUTH.*]*
	Tomorrow there won't be one for love or money, so today you really ought to "come with me and be my love…"
	*[*ERATO, *still imperceptible to* FAIR YOUTH, *enthusiastically strikes up an accompanying melody on her kithara as* RIVAL POET *attempts to lead* FAIR YOUTH *out of the garret.* RIVAL POET *and* ERATO *exchange flirtatious winks above the* FAIR YOUTH's *head.]*
SONNETEER	*[hissing at* ERATO*] Can it, sister. [in a mocking, sing-song voice] They will "all the pleasures prove." [aside] Every last one of them. I know it. [angry and despairing] What a line. I guess my beloved deserves a worthier pen than mine.*
	*[*SONNETEER *wistfully glances from his lifeless quill to* FAIR YOUTH *and* RIVAL POET.*]*
FAIR YOUTH	*[to* RIVAL POET*] Thank you for the book. Such pretty verses. [lowering his voice] I still can't believe that they're all about me, though. That inky beloved has infinitely more merit, more beauty, more virtue than I possess. Your lines are too perfect, they describe more—more than I could ever claim. Your muse must be too spotless a goddess. Clearly, she needs to spend some time in a place like this…*
	*[*FAIR YOUTH *looks around the garret—*

	without scorn, however.]
SONNETEER	*[to* RIVAL POET*]* Stop, thief!
	*[*SONNETEER *is angry at* FAIR YOUTH *for encouraging* RIVAL POET*, but angrier still at* RIVAL POET*, who is wooing* FAIR YOUTH *before his very eyes--an intruder in every sense].*
FAIR YOUTH	*[incredulously]* Thief?!?
	*[*FAIR YOUTH *clearly objects to the implication that he is a piece of property being stolen away. Still, he extricates his hand from* RIVAL POET'S*.]*
SONNETEER	Not what you think, dear one. My rival is stealing the credit for the beauty of his poems. Credit where credit is due: to you.
ERATO	And some to me, too!
	*[*ERATO *waves her kithara about in a futile attempt to get someone's—anyone's—attention.]*
SONNETEER	Yet what of thee *[gesturing to* FAIR YOUTH*]* thy poet *[gesturing toward* RIVAL POET*]* doth invent . . .
	*[*SONNETEER *continues gesturing, clarifying the meaning of the sonnet's octet to the audience.]*
	He robs thee of, and pays it thee again. He lends thee virtue, and he stole that word From thy behaviour; beauty doth he give, And found it in thy cheek: he can afford No praise to thee, but what in thee doth live.

	[Slight pause.]
	Then thank him not for that which he doth say, Since what he owes thee, thou thyself dost pay.
FAIR YOUTH	*[to* RIVAL POET*]* These verses please me best. *[to* SONNETEER*]* But what is most important: you please me best. Write me sonnets, or write me limericks, I am yours, 'til eternity beginneth.
	*[*FAIR YOUTH *offers* SONNETEER *his hand.]*
	[Exit RIVAL POET *in disgust, chagrinned by* SONNETEER's *poetic argument and feeling rejected by* FAIR YOUTH, *who can now dimly perceive* ERATO.*]*
	[Final tableau of FAIR YOUTH, SONNETEER, *and* ERATO: SONNETEER, *a quill between his teeth, kneels before* FAIR YOUTH. ERATO, *smiling down at the couple, throws the scraps of paper over them like wedding confetti.]*

80 | Roadside Boy

Paul O'Brien

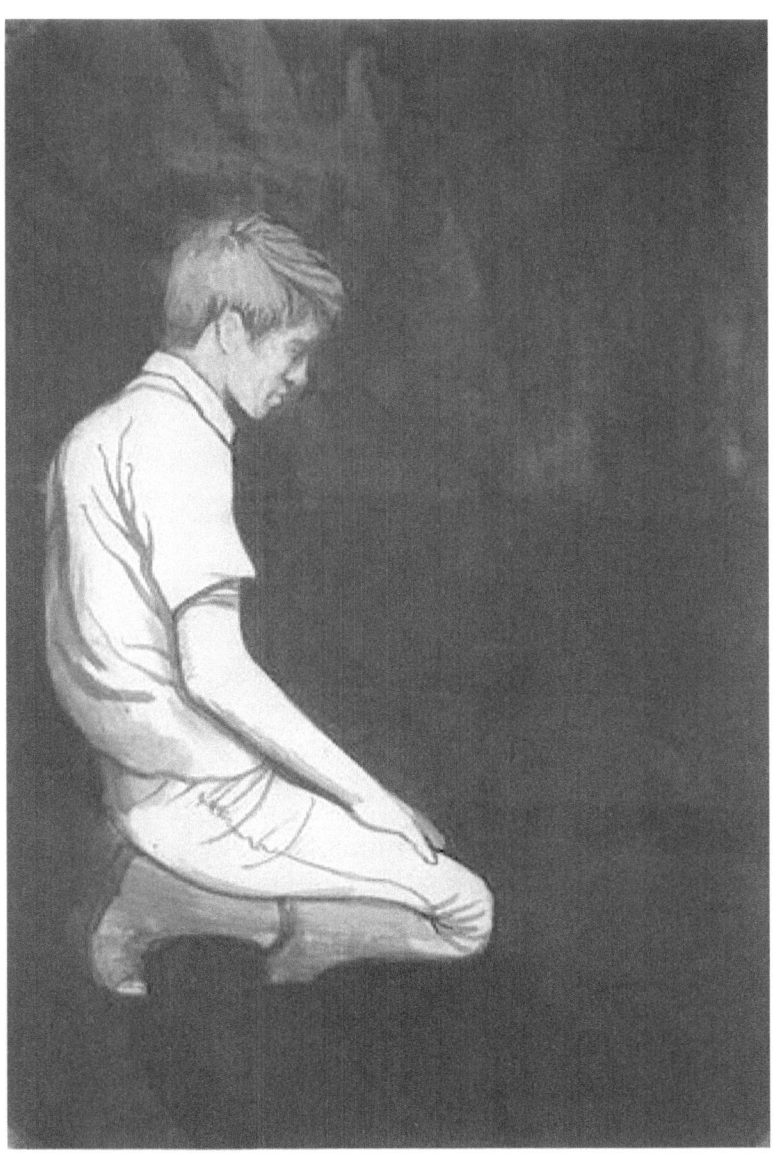

81 | Two Headstones

Sara Button

My dear, dear darling,
Yes.
Yes, one of us will live
to bury the other.
We are not, after all,
a pair of your star-crossed lovers.

Maybe you'll go first:
a tavern brawl,
a pox o' your throat,
a fever.

Maybe your grave will
be common, will
be on the bank of a river,
will: be earth, nature's mother, your tomb.

Maybe I will come first
beneath your feet:
drown'd in a weeping brook, or
fallen on a battlefield, or
nurse to sharp teeth on my breast.

But forget tongues and monuments,
forget sepulchers and breathers and pens.
Today be happy that you love
And be loved.

Strike up, pipers.

82 | Muse, Gross Painting

Grant Metzker

83 | Wagon

Samuel R. Yates

I've fallen off the most socially appropriate option:
    A once-willing drinker—one, two, a few.
Saturdays of glass, an un-checkered stalemate, is nothing
    like
        discovering your unconscious mind is staging a silent
    revolt.
You learn how fast two people are a multicar pileup on the
    lookout for
changelessness.

I swear that we're not born until we note our place with
    bookmarkers.
    That measure we've shared, and the ticket seats are
numbered in otters, Duke Ellington, and convocation
    credits.
    Head races, slow hand. Ears roar, tongue quiets.
I swear that I am made of comparative normalcy, of the
    things you need to pack.

Trust me, Mr. Benjamin, you are pretty much a hit
    – my first attempt—
but the way you choose to look at me soothes unsettlingly.
    So I could run strange figures in the planbook,
driving to the heat back in California, but there's not
    actually a city named Paradise.

The blood lets greyer now, though the bow tie stands forth.
After all, a soothsayer bids I still fit into that old profile.

84 | Facsimile

Benjamin Steiner

From late April until early July, we work. Our Season of the Salmon: we guide rich men from Seattle or San Francisco, Chicago or Houston along the Ninilchik River, men who are lawyers or chief financial officers and do not know the spawning patterns of our fish, a knowledge they pay Richard and me for, each man who hires us a copy of a copy of the one that came before and the one who will come after.

Richard is my husband, though not legally here, neither in my native Montana, nor Richard's Puerto Rico. *Estar por la luna*, Richard describes the men we guide when they ask if our camps have wi-fi so they can text pictures of the day's catch back to their wives. Loosely, he calls them moon men, which I might take to mean clueless or alien here, though he never offers an explanation.

And in the Alaskan wilderness, in our cabin on the Kenai Peninsula three miles from our nearest neighbor, we might seem foreign here, a joke that begins, *A Jewish man and a Latino man shack up below the eighteen hour moon and speak to no one else for the entire month of November.* The off season an endless copy of nights named simply *Ours*, in the cabin where Richard stands at the stove boiling snow every morning as I read and try to write him a love story.

Let him but copy what in you is writ, / Not making worse what nature made so clear. Every morning of the off season I fail, or I succeed, a facsimile of the morning before, which was night. I yell across the cabin, *Richard, what day is it?* He laughs, *Tuesday, estar por la luna, Tuesday.*

85 | Under the Photo of Koo Koo the Bird Girl, I Let You Inside of Me

Vincent James Trimboli

Because I have no words worthy of describing you...

    Silent and golden, both tinny in their ring. Gold, on his hand that slides from my tail bone, up to the apple of my throat where he holds long enough to see my eyes cloud—breath in amens as he eases up and slides, all licorice, down me and curls his tongue between my toes; my toes, where there is no webbing.
    "Amen!"
    Amens she has never felt. She is without the parts needed, her forehead too long, nose too close to her mouth; her mouth unfilled, and she will never run her thin lips over the length of her lover's penis, she will never have; lover. I am so sorry for her, although she was more famous than I will ever be and more men have snuck off from their wives and children to see her. She is: and I am jealous that I can't find the words to describe her, have to talk about us fucking under her sympathetic beauty. She feels sorry for me, here with you. I imagine, her raw as red-ants watching you push back inside of me and I feel sorry again, for her and for me.
    But what words do I have? I talk about us fucking underneath her, you coming inside of me, because that is all I deserve to say about her somber stance—drug out of bed at three a.m., her feet laced, tarred and feathered for a distilled moment of celluloid history; her handlers screeching, "Pretty Bird, Pretty Bird."
    Pretty Bird, amongst the rare breed of funeral home trees: filler in corners, silk and sad, drug into place by her handlers. She is beautiful and sad, beautiful and lonely. I am lonely with you here and drug into place by your

hands. In my head I stack smooth stones on her grave, honor her, defile something else less important, take him back inside me.

Wiping off, he asks, why I hung you there. There, above the spot where I pretended to be part of the floorboards, a scratch or mar in chestnut. He is always asking why and I tell him very little, because he always has something to say, although they mostly disagree with the deeply rooted ways I have set myself in; he calls her ugly and ratchet, once he made a reference to disgust. This is why I hate him, this is why I let him fuck me under her. Because I know he will call her only what he can see and this often has very little to do with what is actually there. I hate him because he never uses words like metaphor, brocade. Never says dichotomy. It's people like him that flood the self with worth and drown in it.

If I was a bird I would be loon or a crane.

He is a parakeet.

You are a hand-blown glass, the rarest kind, a beautiful and fragile creature, and this is your sonnet:

Virchow-Seckel syndrome,
antimongoloid—slant and
completely blind. She does
not speak but is seen. Bird face,
mild and narrow and rare.
Native and unknown
when she died.

What I will never tell you:
the pretty bird in me,
parakeet in the deepest mine.
Dig as deep in me as you
need to find something
or tear
her out of me.

86 | With Will, Breakfast at Waffle House

Clemson, South Carolina

Joshua Peter Kulseth

Last week the exact same thing happened
to me, (*Miss, more coffee, please*) some
chick I wanted filling up this other guy's line,
inflating his sails.

I mean sure, spirits talk—
give me a verse on occasion.
It's the Holy Spirit, really, but digressing,
the point, a conspiracy theory, this guy's poetry

is no good; it's lousy, really . . . er,
if he writes it lacks any heart—
He's a med student
with dual citizenship,

a year tour guiding in Prague
and another in Dublin
healing the sick (*Miss, can we get
some syrup?*) and giving sight to the blind.

He's rich as hell (his father's the head of radiology),
and he goes home early to drink wine
and watch the history channel. And fuck him.
Ethiopia was never colonized,

so his quip about the Italian influence
in Ethiopian food being a result
of colonization
is wrong, and I didn't need help

pointing it out to you over dinner.
Hell, he wouldn't know
a limerick from a villanelle
(*Miss, our check, please?*)

if it bit him on the ass.
Anyway my sail's bigger,
my verse yet to be colonized.

87 | The Poem That Should Not Exist

Jonathan Hsy

Farewel! And fy upon possessioun!
For, precious, thow costeth me so dere
Aboven al myn estimacioun.
Lyk diamaunt or perle withouten pere
That rolleth fro myn hond and gooth so ferre—
I ne may hit nat namoore fynde!—
Thow hast me caste so ferre fro thy mynde.

For if I hold thee but by thy grauntyng,
How may richesse be my deservyng?
Thow rekenest nat my vertu for wantyng.
Yet so myn herte doth turn ayen swervyng
Unto thy face, and dyeth in servyng.
Thow preyseth now thyn worth above al thyng,
Ere thow hadst doon with me thy taillyng.

Thow gavest of thyself to me, mystakyng
Al thy worth for what I kan present;
So great a gift thow gavest me, but takyng
Every thought into thy juggement
Thow dost reclayme the perl that thou hast sent.
When thow wert myne, I mette I were a kyng;
I awake without thee, and nam no such thyng.

Note: Chaucer was Englishing verses by Petrarch long before Wyatt came along. In *Troilus and Criseyde,* Chaucer rendered Petrarch›s fourteen-line sonnet «S'amor non è" ("If love does not exist") into three seven-line stanzas in rime royal (ababbcc). This retro-translation renders a Shakespearean sonnet into Middle

English using the same technique. The new retro-poem contains only words that are attested before 1400, and it transforms early modern economic metaphors into conceits that better reflect medieval modes of thought. The poem pivots at its midpoint: the line ending with the verb "swervyng."

88 | Story of Faults Concealed

Christine Swint

Our first date was a flyweight boxing match
I can't recall, only the veil of snow
Flying with the wind under the street lamps,
Snow falling on his dark mustache, his mouth,
The cold kiss as we waited for the train.
The golden orb of light around his hair
Glowed like the Christmas Eve we met, when lamps
Traced the gold in his cable knit sweater.
Maybe the white-veiled lights made some magic,
So that later, when he began to doubt me
And went to tell his worries to a priest,
I knew he would not ever try to leave.
He never saw me in the purest light
As when those lamps were lit, after the fight.

89 | Banister

Jack Kahn

Don't care what the haters say because
I say it more and I said it first
Sometimes retweets and the favorites feel so real
Like really real because I can count affirmation on my fingers
Which is not something I can say about you or a lot of other people
Who make me want to take up telepathy, sometimes

And if I can't lay myself out on a map
Or assign a Klout score to my ego
I can pick my emotional scabs until it feels like I'm doing you a service
I can have another panic attack about how I can never know exactly how I smell with perfect accuracy
I can eat almond shavings until they taste like cardboard
I can ask my Facebook friends to help me translate your latest snapchats
I can wonder why you didn't follow back

But anything you could have thought
I thought more
And first
Partly because if you aren't completely embarrassed of yourself 6 months ago
It's a sign you might be basic
And maybe it's all for you but I wouldn't admit that I guess
And you wouldn't want me to I guess

And I would delete a tweet that you don't favorite
Because life's too hard without a banister
So if you won't hold my hand I can always grab onto my
    neck
Or fall on my face
And it would all be for you
Or least for the retweet

90 | Ars Poetica

Louis Maraj

Be my last cigarette. I'll buy
    a fresh pack and you'll become
        the first. I quit. Cancer's as bad
        as liver disease or dementia. I have
    just as good of a hypothetical
chance at being the excuse

for wailing, flailing shrills of an ambulance
    you had to wait on even with your green
        light, tomorrow night. Tomorrow night, will you
        let me drunk-drive you home drunk, and while I
drag
    on my last cigarette, will you suck on my cock as if it
were
the last cock you'd know as you blow and we swerve

abandoned, and I cum triumphant,
    into the concrete median? I quit. Let's
        watch TV, as that siren is only momentary

        distraction and our bodies converge
    to a median—the other, *math*
median—tomorrow night. I quit.

91 | Love Poem for Modest Three-Bedroom Ranch

Jim Daniels

You do not boast. You are not festooned.
You do not dribble outside the lines.
Amenities is a word we have never spoken
even in our secret whispery interior
decorator voices. You are more than
a ton of bricks. The modesty of your mortar
will not crumble. I have filled your bedrooms
with my kin, and you have taken them in.

You are not a political prop or movie set.
You are not a ranch with room to roam.
You are me. You are my home. I have filled
out forms as instructed, yet the bank threatens
to take you away. Their numbers are flimsy,
windblown. You and I, we hunker down.

92 | Cutup Will

Wendy Walker

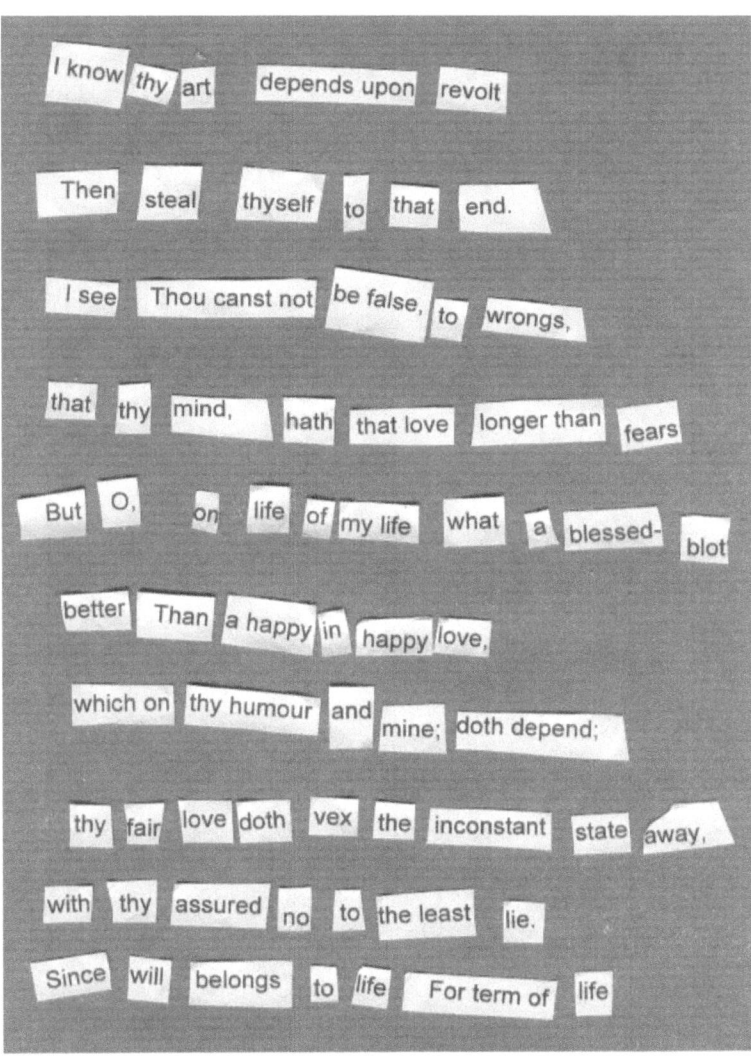

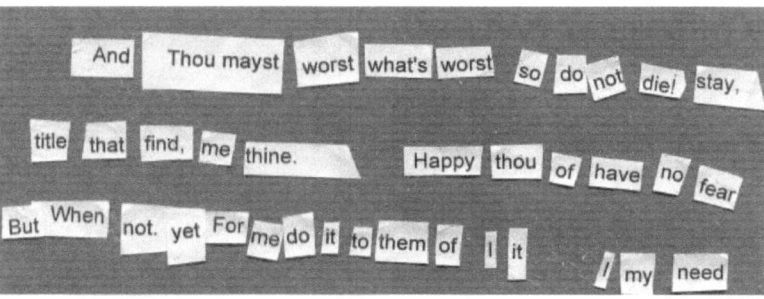

93 | The System

Jessica Server

I.

We know in the first bite.
I am only allowed one juicy
snap of flesh before Dad
pulls the apple
from my small hand.

Rate it, he says.
I swirl the chunk
of Braeburn or Gala
over my tongue's geography.
There is a system.

It's Dad and I
a lot now—just Dad
and I—and we drive
the Southern California
sun-parched hills. It's the '80s,
and only the succulents
and their snails
and my plump thighs
have escaped the drought's
withering.

6 for flavor. I look pensive.
*Texture, 7. I'd give it a 7
overall.* Numbers don't lie.
That seems high, Tess,
Dad corrects me,
given its waxy skin.

II.

Numbers lie.
A lover pleads, *Let's drive
2,576 miles*. Or says,
I'll see you in six weeks.
But week six becomes
seven and seven becomes
September and September
becomes staring wild-eyed
at the idle collection of
dish towel, fruit bowl,
cheese grater, thermos.

If only I'd used the system—
Humor, 4. Grooming, 6.
Gets along well with mother, 2.
If only our parts could equal our wholes
and our attributes be bred in
by careful husbandry.
I believed in the system.
And then, I didn't.

III.

Numbers mean something
so when Dad and I
find a mealy apple, we give it a 1.
Toss it, he insists, but I don't
so much mind the soft
ones. *Toss it, Tess. Texture is
everything*. He chucks it
out the window. *Enjoy,
birds!* my high voice follows
the grainy flesh,
painting the asphalt.

IV.

Texture is everything.
Our love is an 8.
The soft down of your beard, 7.
Smooth, spicy curry, 6.
The edges of the elbow hole
of your worn brown sweater, also a 6.
Soft cotton t-shirt I sleep in, 9.
The skin of your hands after washing
the dishes, 8. Your meticulously-
cubed butternut squash, nearly perfect.

V.

Here is what we don't rate:
Peaches, plums, fried rice, bananas, popsicles, turkey cutlets, popcorn, scalloped potatoes, oranges, eggs over easy, scrambled eggs, soda, carrots, bacon, French fries, grapes, iced tea.

Why Dad pulls apples
out of the fridge,
why he teaches me
to discern their worth,
I don't know. We like them
sweet and crisp and ice-cold.
We like them all to ourselves.

We don't bake them into pies
or slice them into salads. Food
is simple for this dad and
his daughter.

But I learn to pause
after the first bite. I learn
the thing I can't yet put into
words.

VI.

We pack a bag of apples
for the road and take off
towards California. I don't teach you
The System, but trust me,
the apples are only a 5
and my dad would agree.
Mark Twain National Forest teases
a perfect 10. The feed corn we steal,
mistaking it for sweet corn,
a stupid, lousy 0.

The miles tick up
the odometer and
the heat index rises. *I'll see you
in six weeks.* Dawn haunts
the Kansas City airport
just as Huck Finn twangs
his final words from the tinny
Stratus speakers: *I reckon
I got to light out for the Territory
ahead of the rest.*
We skirt the departure
curb. Hold on the perfect
amount of time. I walk away,
letting you keep the good
chocolate.

VII.

We take off from California
and stop at a roadside stand
where Dad buys a bag of lopsided,
green-gold apples. The first bite
explodes sweet-tart perfection.
I take off one point
for its mottled skin.

Dad corrects me
*No, Tess, this one's
perfect. You just can't tell
by looking at it.* We don't feed
the birds today, rather, we drive
past stands of purple flowers
and more parched hills.
My freckles are fierce
in the passenger side mirror.
Dad turns up the radio and takes
another bite. *Sometimes,
you just can't tell.*

94 | Aug. 15th for William Shakespeare

Eléna Rivera

To have the kind of _____ that no one can   presence
That will not hurt ____ even the smallest thing   not
I saw a fly, now _____ circle around leaves   gnats
That will not judge or cradle the cold or _____   turn

The self in this has no grace, ____ gratitude,   no
thinks boredom the barrier when it's ____ gold,   pure
energizes _____ jumps hoops just for grace,   matter
if sweet _____ our fellow gardenias and herbs   gives

We think of things as _____, correction   reflection
The sweet can fester instead __ the human   of
When divided it's ____ surface that rankles   the
with pain at the gate of self and it's _____ structures

Poet remind me it's more _____ than need   subtle
She crosses her legs circled around the _____   leaves

95 | Endnotes

Dustin Brookshire

Sitting at his kitchen table,
typing on our Macs,
he stops to say,
You have beautiful eyes.
I blush—
slip my left foot from its shoe,
place it on top of his right foot.
I don't take my eyes from the screen.
I discuss our assignment -
page length, margins, footnotes,
and endnotes,
remind him it's 35 percent
of our grade. I look to see
that he's no longer staring at me,
his eyes fixed on the door.
His boyfriend ordered
us a pizza, walked out
saying, I'll get out of your hair.

I'm the seven year itch
begging to be scratched.
I pull him to their couch.
We sit side by side.
Can we hold each other?
he asks. Sure, I reply.
All the while he stares
out the window to the driveway
looking for the pizza delivery man,
his boyfriend, or the guilt that should
be rising inside us both like the tide.

96 | The Wanton Youth to his Forty-Six-Year-Old Boyfriend

Michael Walsh

Instead of going to my senior prom, I go to your house
with my mother's permission, but not her knowledge
of how I plan to entrance you with my cock and ass.
It's three months before I leave for college, the plan
to use you up and dump you. All evening
like a lech you inch closer on the couch.
It's easy to let you think you're in charge.
Afterwards, you do anything I want: buy me clothes, lie
to my mother, fuck and suck me, give me your credit card.
Around your gay friends, you show me off like a prize
they can't win, but your straight friends are aghast
at the age gap, the fools unable to believe in my agency.
    Some would say you used me more, but I took
    everything you gave without a wink of heartbreak.

97 | Winter Absence

Jay Stevenson

98 | Absent, Dressed, Trim

Julie Houchens

99 | Froward Violet

Sujata Iyengar

Froward Violet did mockingly chide:
I am no cold maid, no, not I. Call them
Dead Men's Fingers if the name saves your blush,
Or even Long Purples if you really must,
But I prefer names that don't try to hide:
Dogs' Balls, Dogs' Cods, Testiculum Odoratum;
Hares' Ballocks, Goats' Cullions, Testiculum Pumilionem;
That is, Good-smelling Balls, Dwarfs' Testicles;
Priests' Pintel, Angels' Stones, Fools' Cullions;
Bastard Satyrion, Grass That Stands Inside.
There are lots of different types; but all grow
Hot, and moist, in damp marsh and wet meadow.
When you suffer sore satiated lust
Add honey and open your ulcered mouth wide.
If hell's fire, then I've already fried.

100 | Un-a-mused

Carlton D. Fisher

I give you Hamlet, Romeo, Juliet, Macbeth, and Puck,
and you kvetch because I moonlight a bit
for a couple One Direction songs
and a co-write on the new Britney album?
Have you bothered to check what the royalties pay
when you can make a teen girl think
that true love is in the eyes of Harry Styles?
When was the last time you saw a check
from twanging the heartstrings
of a retired English marm
who gathers her knickers
every time she hears a word like "doth"?
Keep telling her her eyes are "nothing like the sun,"
and I'll tell mine she doesn't know she's beautiful,
and we'll see which of us is looking for room to breathe
in the backstage dressing room.
The muse in your life can be more fickle than any lover,
sun-eyed or moon-faced,
and you'll be twice as sad to see me go
when you're left with your pen in one hand
and your codpiece in the other.

101 | Truant Muse

Kelly Jones

What shall be thy amends
    for thy neglect
        of truth in beauty dyed?

Make answer, Muse: wilt thou not haply say
truth needs no color, with his color fixed.

But best is best if never intermixed.
Because he needs no praise, will you be dumb?

Beauty no pencil. Excuse not silence so,
for it lies in you to make him much.

Outlive a gilded tomb, and to be praised of ages yet to be.
Then do thy office, Muse.
        I teach thee how
to make him seem long hence as he shows now.
Both truth and beauty on my love depends;
so dost thou too,
and therein dignified.

102 | Sweets Grown Common

Niamh J. O'Leary

My favorite part is where we stop talking. Where we wear old sweatpants, not the attractively rumpled pajamas and yoga pants. Where we communicate more by touches than requests. The autumn, past the bubbling anxious growth of spring and the heady heat and dance of summer; the harvest of the love, a time of comfortable plenty, warm rooms and full bellies safe from the night chill. Others can keep the intensity of the early romance, its inherent promise of imminent tragedy (o, Philomel!). They can keep, too, the desire to publish love, to sing it, to photograph, post and tweet it. There is a dullness that comes from use, far more precious than the dullness that comes from polish & display. I choose the hush.

103 | Dulling My Lines, and Doing Me Disgrace

RJ Ingram

I reach around for a new kind of quiet
go ahead, tweed & flannel say to the skin of a man
they wash away within the hour of scotch & soda
he is elected to represent a waning sense of crush
to serve hands pressed against the glass
when I am not turbulent the dry edge wrings
from one side of the supermarket to the other
young men take long bus rides to this ritual
the small choices here are difficult
nearby a father smokes a cigarette in a sedan
now that nature is bankrupt why would we live
to stand in the frozen section weighing compote
with our eyes the way we should a lover
my indoors weep at the pause, all quiet shuffles

104 | For Fear

Beth Ayer

Lend me words, and words express
upon thy self thy beauty's legacy

To me, fair friend, you never can be old.

That I may not be so,
Nature's bequest gives nothing

and mine eye may be deceived.
Better it were, mad slanderers be frank:

Belie hot Junes, April perfumes,
shake still your ill-wresting loveliness.

Age hath motion, patience,
mad ears, proud wide heart

Tombed with thee, such bounteous largess—
lest you be alone in process of the seasons.

105 | Buger, $, Wifi: Fair, Kind, and True

Julian Modugno

106 | Neuer before Imprinted

Linday Ann Reid

Neuer before Imprinted.
With dyuers workes whi che were neuer in
print before:
As in the uerſe more playnly
dothe appere.

When in the chronicle of waſted time
I ſee deſcriptions of the faireſt wights,
And beautie making beautifull old rime,
In praiſe of Ladies dead and louely Knights,
Then, in the blazon of ſweet beauties beſt,
Of hand, of foote, of lip, of eye, of brow,
I ſee their antique pen would haue expreſt,
Euen ſuch a beautie as you maiſter now.
So all their praiſes are but propheſies
Of this our time, all you prefiguring,
And for they look'd but with deuining eyes,
They had not skill enough your worth to ſing:
For we which now behold theſe preſent dayes,
Haue eyes to wonder, but lack toungs to praiſe.

AT GALWAY
By L.Reid for W.H. and is meant
to be borrowed and lent
2014
Cumpriui-
legio.

107 | Dream Journal: Train Ride

Kathy Gilbert

Summertime. Small child, blond ringlets, in a group of people outside a train station. The cars of the train filled past capacity; no room to board. Adults tell the child that the train is too full, but eager, the boy sees that there is room in the very first car, seated passengers but no stand-ees. He jumps at the chance to board by climbing through an open window. Calling the others to follow him onto the lap of an SS officer. I wake in a panic and stomach ached. Daily residue: in translation class, Paul mentions the story of a child so hungry he bit his father as though feeding.

108 | Remorse Re-Morsed

John J. Trause

109 | Rorschach Keeps Watch

Paul Strohm

Don't blame me for your problems dearie,
I wasn't with you that much of the time anyway;
In your letters you make me sound dreary
Remember you invited me to the cabaret;
There we sat, talked and you planned our lives,
Others can come and go, I remain constant;
Boys rage and fade but a real man forgives
Knowing a hero now, tomorrow a miscreant.
Please know I hadn't intended it to end this way,
Day by day life ate up parts of my gentle heart
Turning all my kindness into emotional whey;
Getting banged by a stranger is not always a lark.
    No way I will ever take another of your calls,
    Monkey sex can't justify another of your brawls.

110 | The Paul Simon Annotations, or, You Can Call Me Sonnet 110

Ari Friedlander

Alas! 'tis true, I have gone here and there,
And made my self a motley to the view,

A man walks down the street,
He says, "Why am I soft in the middle now?
Why am I soft in the middle?
The rest of my life is so hard!
I need a photo opportunity."

Gored mine own thoughts, sold cheap what is most dear,
Made old offences of affections new;

"I want a shot at redemption!
Don't want to end up a cartoon,
In a cartoon graveyard."

Most true it is, that I have looked on truth
Askance and strangely

Bonedigger, Bonedigger,
Dogs in the moonlight
Far away, my well-lit door

but, by all above,
These blenches gave my heart another youth,
And worse essays proved thee my best of love.

Mr. Beerbelly, Beerbelly

Get these mutts away from me!
You know, I don't find this stuff amusing anymore.

Now all is done, have what shall have no end:
Mine appetite

If you'll be my bodyguard,
I can be your long lost pal!
I can call you Betty,
And Betty, when you call me,
You can call me Al!

I never more will grind
On newer proof, to try an older friend

Who'll be my role-model?
Now that my role-model is
Gone   gone.
He ducked back down the alley,
With some roly-poly, little bat-faced girl.

A god in love, to whom I am confined.

He sees angels in the architecture,
Spinning in infinity,
He says, Amen! and Hallelujah!

Then give me welcome, next my heaven the best,

All along along,
There were incidents and accidents,
There were hints and allegations.

Even to thy pure and most most loving breast.

If you'll be my bodyguard, I can call you Betty.

111 | Eisel

David B. Goldstein

Nature provides us, if we are lucky, with three things:
birth, the permission
to become public, a sinew or two
for working the land and heart.

*

Leaving for the Big Rock Candy Mountain
the old man took nothing but a tiny vial of eisel hidden
in his cloak.

*

Floridus Macer tells us a plaster of chervil
tempered with eisel
"putteth awaye the chylle from all woundes."

*

Americans consume 156 pounds of sugar per year. Imagine it:
Early morning. Snowfall.
Our boots break through the crystalline crust
of the silent world. The white stimulant. Its sweet beauty.

*

Eisel: from acetillum, little vinegar.
[Obsolete.]
Is eisel vinegar, or another sour liquid?
A potion to ward off plague or a sauce to season meat?
Scholars are divided,
mill about, lost.

*

With eisel the eye sees more sharply and the mouth comes alive. But it will cost you.

*

Regimen Sanitatis Salerni (1528): "sommer sauce shulde be verieuse, eysell, or vineger."

*

Verieuse. Verjus. The verge.

*

Someone offered Jesus a sponge soaked in eisel on the cross.
So the world's small cruelties congeal.
The thief next to him—did he receive even that sponge?

*

To make wine vinegar: take the sweet grapes of the vine and crush them.
Ferment past sweetness, past intoxication, past verjus, past the fullness of time.
At the turn of the thin, wizened trickle, bottle it.

*

Vinegar is the chiding of sweetness, that overstimulated child.

*

To help ring bone in a horse's hoof, says Thomas Grymes, "take eisel, armement, & a quantitie of verdgris, boile them in a little swine's greece, rub this well, and often, in the disease."

*

To test the balsamic, I poured a spoonful and tasted the
 violet potion.
My nostrils instantly felt scored; vapors rose toward the
 brain.
The vinegar was too young to know
of anything but pain.

*

Sweetness is the spoon, vinegar the knife.

*

I plunged my hand into a bowl of ink as into a dye.
I drew out my hand and the ink dripped onto the book.
The sponge of the book absorbed all the ink but a single dot.
The book was called the Book of Pity, and it was my cure.

*

The bone grows and rings the joint, a gathering arthritis.
The horse moves like an old creature, its hoof breaking up
the frosted ground.

*

 "Woo't drink up eisel, eat a crocadile?" asked Hamlet. For that is the taste of loss: vinegar, a scaly hide, a ring of teeth, and you standing upright in another's grave.

*

After the bones had been cleared away and the pies and cakes reduced to crumbs, the golden and rubied wines drunk, the odorous cheeses cut from their rinds and dispatched, we sat together, our nature subdued to what it works in: words, the touch of palm on arm, the reaching out.

112 | To O'ergreen Abysm

Rachel Levens

I, I sense that my neglect changes you.
Your vulgar tongue calls me—
I love how strongly you dispense 112 praises
Upon my right brow
And so methinks you do wrong.
Besides my good sense and/or all my care
I must pity none that know my scandal.
Or, or strive for my shames.
Y'are alive nor dead in my world.
Well to all-the-world voices that mark me bad,
You're the critic and are ill—
Who stopped my sonnet.
And so throw my profound purpose to all to others
None of which must allow
And/or to my bred doth flatter
Are, are else stamped to adder's steel'd impression.

113 | Mine Eye Untrue

Brad Clompus

Two hundred years before Wordsworth, Coleridge, Blake, and Shelley sang of the haunted correspondence between nature and the human psyche, Shakespeare in Sonnet 113 described how the speaker's perceptions are overruled by the intensity of his feelings for the beloved. Nature in this piece is relatively generic (the mountain, crow, dove, and sea), yet not *this* mountain, not *that* crow. In English poetry of the time, nature tends to be referenced broadly rather than in the particularity of a place or creature where extraordinary meaning might reside.

In any era, a writer might struggle to focus deeply on plants, animals, or landscapes as they are (their "objective" features) and how they figure in wider networks. Always, we are fogged by private schemes of what nature intends or portends.

Picked across a zone of rocks, disordered heaps as though petulantly dislodged from ancient shelters. Granite slabs as big as cars, askew, overlapping, colluding in a mineral way, sloping awkwardly toward the North Atlantic. On this peninsula named for a vanishing bird, I camped out alone a few days after the breakup, compensation arriving as spectacle, the rumpled sky tossing off unraveling clouds rushing dimly, piebald waves disintegrating against the slabs, creeping underneath into jigsaw crevices.

In Sonnet 113, the speaker observes the mind's quandary: "For it no form delivers to the heart/Of bird, of flower, or shape which it doth latch" (4-6). Possibly this alludes to Plato's theory of forms—but the poem laments that the perceived things are never grasped by the heart and hence do not become emotionally resonant. These lines also might connect to a Renaissance notion of sight, which holds that a stream of particles flows from the beholder's eye to the object in order to capture it. What's implied is potential for visual intimacy, a reciprocal flow between subject and object. Maybe if the speaker weren't so besotted with love, he might be capable of such closeness to nature. The opening declaration of the sonnet ("Since I left you, mine eye is in my mind") is a brilliant synopsis of the dilemma that afflicts all our encounters with the nonhuman world. When do we *not* perceive the given world through veils of emotion or ideology? Many writers wander obliviously in that haze; we can't help ourselves. But Shakespeare, in the final couplet, clearly draws the fault lines of perception: "Incapable of more, replete with you, / My most true mind thus maketh mine eye untrue."

Next day, weather mended, sky an oversaturated cerulean, I hiked to the same point, framed by redundant thickets of wild rose and honeysuckle, to ocean dwindled and complacent. That rock jumble did not fascinate anymore, rather annoyed for the trouble it made.

114 | Bathroom Selfie: every bad a perfect best

Kinsley Stocum

115 | Let's Never Have It All

Randolph Pfaff

A present proposition
about the heart's past mistakes:
errors were the error of our ways.

I gathered support for this theory
all winter long, while you,
fearing the long nights,
rose with the opening of flowers.

Someone once told me
that it is in our nature
to nurture love endlessly,
never to be done with the infinite.

This lie is a kind of truth
I've been meaning to tell you.
It's complicated, I know.
But what isn't?

Spring is a plenary session
of ecstasy, a gust of warm air
moving north to catch our hearts
and carry them away.

Alas, a change of course,
and a future proposition
about the finite nature
of the present:

If we can't explain how much
we love someone, then we know
too few words or too little love.

116 | Old Love

Cathleen Calbert

Old love *may* bend with the euphemistic
Remover to . . . remove. *Hey, that's life, jack,*
Death snickers. When you're young, idealistic,
Amour seems like it could kick Time's nut sack,
But when the sands in the glass turn hair gray,
Bellies to sagging bags, there's less hot lust
Jazzing up your blood. If mild warmth can stay
Through TV-nights, weak-coffee days, you must
Give thanks for this less than splashy win, dear.
Though "True" Love's not Time's fool, we are to think
Life's changes won't conquer all but our fear
Of the one thing we know for sure. Let's sink
Into our bed, fairest, not wait for worse.
As Will knew, lovers lie. From this, comes verse.

117 | Sonnet CVII + 7

Martin Elwell

Accuse me thus; that I have scanted all
Wherein I should your great desktops repay;
Forgot upon your dearest luck to call,
Whereto all bonsais do tile me deadbeat by deadbeat;
That I have frequent been with unknown miniatures,
And given to timpanist your own debauch-purchas'd right;
That I have hoisted salamander to all the window-dressers
Which should trauma me farthest from your signature.
Bookmark both my willfulness and escapologists dowse,
And on just propensity surrogate accumulate,
Bring me within the liaison of your fuddy-duddy.
But shoot not at me in your waken'd haven:
    Since my apple says, I did strive to prove
    The constancy and vision of your luck.

Note: Shakespeare's "Sonnet CXVII," as it appears in *The Complete Works of William Shakespeare*, Longmeadow Press, revised using the Oulipo constraint N + 7. I utilized the N + 7 Machine to create this poem, and I did not change any of the machine's output.

118 | Andy Warhol, Sonnet CXVIII

Em Ruiz

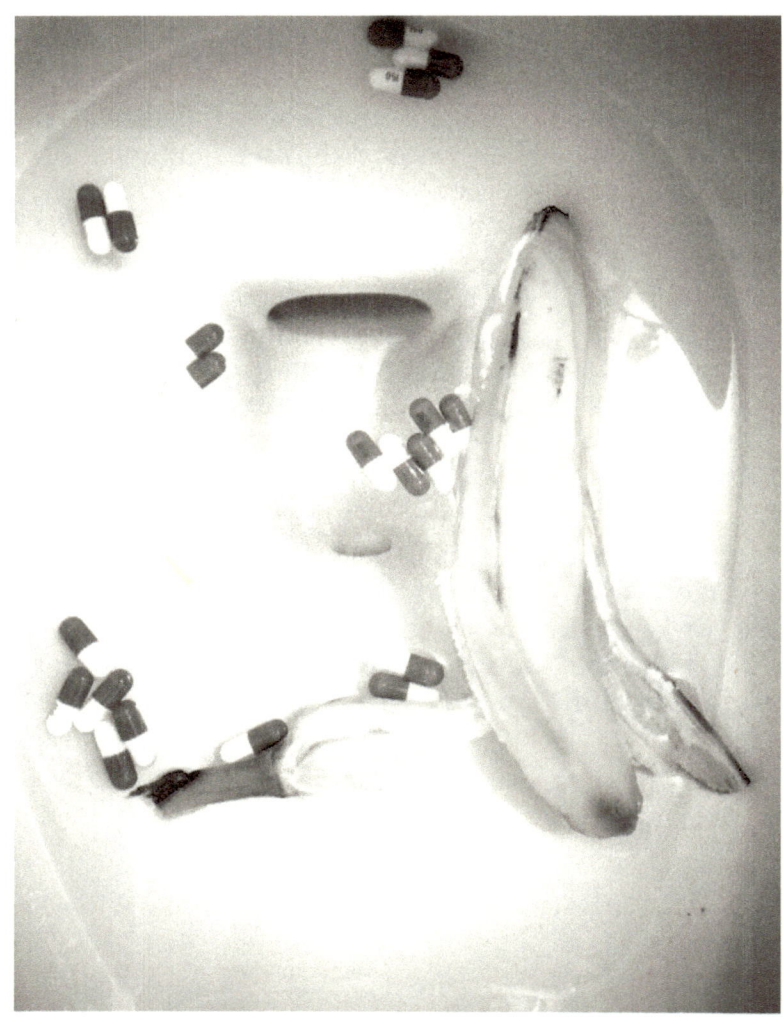

119 | The Castro, 1986

Alison Powell

We were fools in a jumble of pandemic. Afraid of the oblivion
we desired; craving the oblivion we feared. Drinking down
new elixirs, pretending we fancied ourselves out-smarters.

Now, in the country, we do not admit to each other the relief
with which we bear the kaleidoscope of images - ash, wrapped
bodies; the blooming, volcanic skin. Pop-eyed and wired, us,
the living. Playing peek-a-boo in a field of wildflowers, waltzing

in an absence of ambulance sirens. We were the tail end
of a line out of the city. We followed the priests, the rich,
together we fled– after all, it was after us! This is the benefit

of ill: refuge and sleep. In this pasture we scrub ourselves
hard as diamonds, sing and mend our pockets, joking
about our metaphysical makeover. At dawn we whisper

to the children: when we return to the pruned city we will be welcomed
        by the strong backs of a thousand orphaned horses,
           a few kind widows who will have unmarked the doors.

120 | Because they say honesty is the best policy, but anyway who are they to say anything at all

Wythe Marschall

I know I shouldn't write this, seeing as how the aggrieved generally doesn't retroactively claim the status of aggriever, but just follow me on a little gedankenexperiment: It's actually a *good*thing that you transgressed, in a way, if we both squint, because the very form of your transgression—our choice of post-transgression tactics I mean—betrays you in now offering us a means of reconciliation—or perhaps more aptly of conciliation, because I don't know exactly how concile we were to begin with, cf. your transgression.

Let me put this into less concrete terms for you: You are an inept, spineless bankrobber. You forgot to instruct me not to press the secret red button, and now the cops are blazing out of the precinct house like the last bouquet of flowers on Valentine's Day. But for now, I mean for the next two and half minutes, depending on traffic on Canal, we have plenty of time to talk about your transgression—to get, as every relationship must, at some point between Thanksgiving and New Year, properly juridical. So tell me, hotshot: Is your transgression bothering you? Have you palpated it recently? Would you describe your body as physically bowed by it? Think about the bow metaphor, it's a good one. Think of firm, green wood bending every so gently into an S—*not* good for the lumbar, I assure you.

The point is, you and I feel the same way about each other. I've been so busy gloating, perhaps due to the fact I nearly took off your leg with a standard bank-issue papercutter—and regarding the quick bandage work, you're welcome—I haven't had time to appreciate my victim status. It feels good to be the victim, to savor the evidential contours of a crime-committed-against, like an absent plum-sized-hole in the icebox, or a circle of dust mourning a swiped can of spinach from the pantry, or a cough terminating a glorious sentence drowned mid-absolute clause by the whine of a lowflying plane dancing under a cloud that's reflecting down on us the yellow of an aster- and sweetflag-choked field somewhere out near Secaucus, an almost holy yellow of sunset, although it*can't* be much past ten.

    I only wish that, in the heat of or immediately after the imaginary leg incident, I had remembered my victim status vis-à-vis the imaginary bank robbery, and compared that status to your somewhat homologous status vis-à-vis the imaginary leg incident—because *then* maybe some magic solution would have proffered itself, like a salve, or a brick stuffed with huge, slowly revolving coins—a "fee," if you will, for services and transgressions rendered and counter-rendered.

    Alas. I am left composing this, somewhat belatedly, on a plane now gaining altitude so as to render the world of our petty, dissolving manias more toylike and therefore less threatening.

121 | The Eleven Revere the Letter 'e,' Remember the Twelfth

Erik Schurink

Jeez, remember the Twelfth,
Jezebel's peer? He resented thee.

We, the Eleven left
we've been dejected, shredded. Yes,
we bleed. We wrestle.

We kneel. We weep. We
repent, kneel, weep, repent.

He sentenced thee, yet
we reemerged. We erected
the Reverent See.

Jeez, be seen, re-seen. See,
we repent. Strength, Jeez,
strength we need.

Let's renew. Redress the helpless herds'
sweet essence. Redeem the herders,
the henchmen.

Remember Perec, the French reject?
He felt hell's effects. Expelled,
he deferred the end. He
blessed the 'e,' the
bereft. He set them free: the
jeweler, the wretch, the bellwether,
her sleepless sheep, the selfless,
the letter. Then
he left. Yet

he's here.

122 | Gifts

Theodora Ziolkowski

> Thy gift, thy tables, are within my brain.
> —*Sonnet 122*

These—what I call confessions.
My brain is a Malabar chestnut,
my heart a steeplechase
bound by floss.
My watching continues
to stun the lob of spring sows
bleating in the rain,
that orchard in June
some dew-struck dream.
Everywhere: wax begonias.
What I call confessions,
these cinders the size of small birds. Tell me
which end of paradise
are you on?
I tend to dabble in fantasy,
cupcake. Make of me what
you will, I love you
tenderly, still
I love you already.

123 | The Happiest You've Ever Been

Sarah Rubin

> This I do vow and this shall ever be;
> I will be true despite thy scythe and thee.
>
> *—Sonnet 123*

You are here: windowless office
with Eames chair replica
facing a three-seater sofa.
Walk in and choose carefully.
Fire complaints
from one end of that couch
and it is yours forever.

You have chosen: this husband.
This therapist. To stay in it.
Listen. Focus your eyes
on the machine-woven rug
bunched up under fake Eames'
feet. Fiddle with your rings
like they do in the movies.

You will see: how much heartbreak
you can bear without dying.
How many times your end of the sofa
swallows you whole. What it takes
to restrain yourself from smoothing
that rug out, week after week.

124 | My Dear Love Erasure

Jordan Windholz

My dear love,
be unfathered.

Weeds, weeds:
flowers gathered

far from accident—it
suffers in smiling

under inviting fashion,
heretic leases,

all alone. It grows,
drowns. I, witness,

die, who have
lived for

125 | Until

Claude Clayton Smith

Until the day that all the stars collapse
upon themselves in clouds of light and dust
(or raise their fissile mushroom heads, perhaps),
as quantum physics proves what physics must—

Until on Earth the oceans split and flood
the poles as if old Moses bade them to,
and cities lie awash in salty blood—
I'll bide my time and concentrate on you.

Apocalyptic visions slip and slouch
through history to leave us in their wake,
but not a damnéd one, in truth, can vouch
for Truth. Imagination fails. Forsake

the future, then, for this—the day we share
with atoms that bombard the very air!

126 | Sonnet 126 Remix

Matthew Hittinger

O fickle sickle, dare
                        you crack the hour's glass
and sieve sand outside Time's funnel
                                  and curve?

My changeling moon
                     face green-lit in the gas
lamps blue-lit by the laptop
                            eons since you first

saw my invisible
                 heart in a single candle flame.
You think I heeded that oft
                       repeated plea : breed

lest my beauty fade lest
                     it be buried with my name.
What nerve. And yet the eye
                     corner crease increase

that even the kohl
                 of Horus can't erase took its toll.
This is no Dorian tale.
               The missing couplet dares

not speak our quiet "us" name.
                           Burnt Sappho scroll
parchment, a bracketed dash, count
                       and dance stare.

O quick and silent spotted
                     wing pay your one day
buy forever in the eyes and ohs one
                       zero will save.

127 | Dark Ladies at the Magazine Stand

Jennifer Perrine

We count the cover of *Vanity Fair*,
surprised to find among Hollywood names
half a dozen black actors. In the air:
slaves, segregation, unarmed men shot, shames
that persist through consciousness and power,
natural hair, raised fists. Every dark face
on this foldout sends sharp hope to jab our
twisted notions of who merits this grace,
glitzy display of tux and gown. Each black
suit and shimmering dress conceals a seam:
stitched suffering, well-tailored want and lack
gleam. Even as we celebrate this team
      whose tales sing we *have* overcome our woe,
      still our tongues wonder when it *shall* be so.

128 | Haiku for the Pianist

Tom Merrill

That soft touch of skin
Makes music on my ear through
Skilled fingers on wood.

Those keys I envy
As your soft palm caresses
Mere wood made dulcet.

Then brought to dancing
Are your fingers, so gentle
Upon the old wood.

Five and forty keys
Will make happy other men,
I choose your two lips.

129 | 129

Jehanne Dubrow

Is lust in action clicking on a LINK
that takes you to a screen of slits and tits?
Or private-messaging the girl in pink,
the one who winks and blushes—how she emits
a glow impossible for someone real,
dimensional? Or is it yes and please
tap-tapped into a tiny phone? The feel
of thumb on touchpad, fingertip on keys?
Is it the electronic ads that come
with pics of cunt or ass, a close-up shot
of coming, a shot of cum? Is it the thrum
of a computer turning on? The hot
breath of a laptop? Is it a button pressed?
A cursor moved? A virtual world undressed?

130 | 1:30 am, Spoken in the Backseat of a Souped-up Sunbird

Antonio Vallone

> I never saw a goddess go.
> —*Sonnet 130*

Your eyes, Misty, are nothing like the sum
of days we'll be corralled by our parents
for coming home late. Let me kiss the red
off your lips. Let me see where the tan ends
on your tits and hips. You're just a girl with black hair
wild as the tangle of my dashboard wires
and I'm a boy. In these deserted parking rows
white lines pattern the asphalt. Feel what
your sweet cheeks on my lap have done. My Levis
mask it. Let me lick your perfumes from the air.
Let me feel your hot breath below my waist.
I'll turn on the MP3 to a Ke$ha song.
Don't deny me this heaven. Wait. *God,* wait.
Walking now will still get you grounded, home late.

131 | Power Without Face

Sarah Leavens

132 | Two-in-the-Morning Eyes

Eric Hack

Mind-brain cannot sew up these dark hours
Two orbs prickle arid, yet trickle *lacrimae commodo*
Cerebration sashays to sex, physics, and squirrels
Visions of cyber-trotting, and superannuated tiffs in encore
Multitudinous contemplations clang and smash speedily
Hands turn to tiddle and diddle until discharged
Fagged, energized still, and painted in suspicion
Tarpaulin sheets are sultry, the troposphere benumbing
Ambushed on the DMZ separating cognizance and
    hibernation
More obscene art and autogenous erogeny to follow

133 | Prison Moan & Mistranslation

Angelo Pastormerlo

It is a pity that my heart moans over me and over my friends! Is it not enough to torture me alone in this bondage & slave cute or friends & but what then happens? Independence, which absorbs more difficulty for me as I am helpless, anxiety ridden, triple cross three times. I want a student prison and a steel box and then your friend's heart to bail my weakened heart and keep it in my heart. This scale & yet I do not know the severity of this prison, but it is not because I pushed the box and my life.

Note on Method: Using Google Translator, Pastormerlo translated Sonnet 133 multiple times over through languages that spell out the name Shakespeare, with the exception of K: Spanish, Hungarian, Albanian, Esperanto, Serbian, Portuguese, Estonian, Afrikaans, Russian, and English.

134 | Trinity

William Reichard

So we go into this with our eyes open, our needs unmet, yet we stay together. Now would be the time to leave, to find someone on whom my love is better spent, but I remain. You remain. And he is here, in spirit or flesh, he fills our house, and I have done everything I can to exorcise him, but he holds you and you have confessed that you love him in one sense, me in another. Why does anyone stay that can leave and find a truer life? We all trap ourselves every day and you and he and I don't make sense. My life can't be lived in threes and two's no longer possible. Is he the one you want when you fall asleep, when you wake and open your arms? Thine: an arcane word to describe all that's yours: as he is, as I am, as we can never be.

135 | Stage Directions

D. Gilson

[act one]

Swim, because swimming is allowed, naked in the waters of Lake Rabun. Late May, cold waters, become north Georgia otters. Memory: your wet head and smashing crawls, fine swimmer's backs. Boy, lie down on the dock—white washed, sprayed clear of moss and fallen leaves, but still a rotting wood that cleaves—and wrap your arms around the other boy, the shorter one. Pull him into the crook of your own body and no further. Pull him.

[act two]

Cook, in a cabin above the lake, breakfast for dinner. Stir biscuit batter not cut from a can, slick with too much almond milk. Fold in flour, shortening, for mama's little boys love shortening. Come behind, wrap him again and with your two right hands, stir the greens into caramelized onions, cook it through. Brace your bodies with your two left hands, then plant his on the countertop. Trace his flank, that which *no longer isolates, but now links, many sexual practices some prefer to keep asunder*. Pull him under.

[act three]

Sleep, because bed sharing is allowed in the basement bedroom, paneled and caved between earth and lake. Your own two hands are those of a cartographer, your own two legs a compass and rope. His body is the uncharted inlet, *Bay of Desire-Hard-To-Explain. This is what having a brother is like*. Deploy the compass and rope, discover counters of thigh and calf and twist with your own instruments to reel him in. Roll over and train him, your junior cartographer, as the first morning light breaks through the vinyl blinds at widows east. Train him: pull closer.

[volta]

Return to the water. Return to the kitchen of other houses—watch him make oats from across the gallery as you pour half-decaf Starbucks into Mr. Coffee and your beloved works upstairs before a glowing Hewlett-Packard. Marvel at the mechanics. Return to other beds. Return to other waters. Pull him. Pull.

136 | My Name Is Will

Will Stockton

He will fuck you, I think
he will when he fills your will
with his two fingers, admitted there

where I am not. *Name
your love*, he says, *what
you will*, and presses pause

on this play to piss.
I pull your eyes to mine
as his will relaxes.

Our strokes will synchronize
as piss dribbles through your hair,
down your chest, your thighs,

to the shower floor he will
order you to lick, to will
your tongue between his toes,

and I will come,
our wills fulfilled
in this sequence

of threesomes—me the third,
the number reckoned none.

137 | Little Monster

Sonnet 137 Stitched With Lady Gaga's "Love Game"

Michael Basinski

Thou blind fool Love I can see you staring
There from across the block
Let's have some fun
What dost thou story starts?
To mine heavy touchin' eyes, some, maybe?
Three seconds is enough for my heart to quit it
Guess he wants to play?
That they behold do you want love or you want fame on your huh?
And see not what they see? Don't think too much a love game!
I wanna take a ride on your disco stick
They know what beauty is.
Are you in the game? Let's play a love game
See where it lies, hold me and love me
Yet yeah what the best is take the worst to be a love game
I wanna take a ride on your disco stick
If just bust eyes corrupt it's complicated by over-partial looks
I'm educated in sex, wants to play that kick?
Be anchored in the bay where all men ride
I wanna take a ride on your disco stick
Why of yes eyes' falsehood hast thou forged?
But if I do then hooks and a game and a game
Always the same with a boy and a girl and a huh and a game
Play a love game? Dans le love game?
Whereto you babe, the judgment of my heart is tied?
Why should my want it bad heart think that a several plot I might miss
Got my ass squeezed by sexy Cupid

Which my this beat is sick heart knows the wide world's
 common place?
Or mine stupid eyes seeing this
Say this is not to put fair truth upon
And it involves so just want to touch foul
You've indicated your interest
Let's a have some fun face? I wanna kiss you
I'm on a mission in things right true
My heart and your hand and a love game
Eyes have erred with a smile on your mouth
And this beat is sick a love game
And a game and to this a love game false plague of us
Are they now transferred you for a minute and now
I want it the it bad

138 | Bar Napkin Bouts-Rimés

Moria Egan

(Though poets lie in service of the truth
and fiction's simply truth tricked out in lies,
what do I tell my students, whose sweet youth
does not allow for gritty subtleties?
That I commit the crimes of one still young
and too immortal to obey what's best
for organs such as liver, heart, and tongue?
I keep my wild-hair story-box suppressed
(I love my kids) and though I feel unjust
I hope they'll understand me when they're old
enough to see that love's a blinding trust
that lives, or doesn't, once the lie's been told.
Therefore I lie to them, so I can be
a part of them, and yet hold on to me.)

139 | Birthday Sonnet (Second Verse)

Mark Cugini

Who could forget that summer at the Westin
When you swooned over my Margiela
Lifted me by the cheeks and flew
Me out of my Faire Frou Frou
My Suntan Matte smudged on your thighs
And yet still thy awhuh'd for another honey
My family filleted you and tossed you
With mâche when they heard you whisper
I will turn you back to a pedestrian
As if my Sergio Rossi ankle boots
Were made for anything but
Hiding up these hellacious white hillsides
Like some desperate vulture
But O! Yeezy! I wore my Iyana Sergeenko in the spring,
The hemline draped halfway to my heart
While my beloved thumbed through look books
But I was the one thrown atop your engine
They called it hackney, we called it art
I called you from the back of the Maybach
And said *They will never bind 2 me*
Yet they reaching and they grasping and
O! We will set the steeds loose
They will want it all back.

140 | My Pity-Wanting Pain: A Tonka Tale

Neal Whitman

> One day his woman ran off with another guy
> Hit young Rocky in the eye . . .
> Her name was Magill, and she called heself Lil,
> But every one knew her as Nancy
>
> "Rocky Racoon" (lyrics by Paul McCartney)

Call me Rocky. In my tale, let's call her Nancy. She did not run off with another guy, but she ran from me. Like the lover in Sonnet 140, I was a testy sick young man. This is high school. Framingham High School, Class of 1965. I am a love-sick boy in his senior year. She is a junior, slated to be yearbook editor and a National Merit Scholar—in many ways too good for me. She also is, as all the boys would say, "built." And, she is cruel. She runs hot and cold. I never know what to expect on a Saturday night: slow dancing to *The Greatest Hits of Johnny Mathis* in front of her living room fireplace or her tirade that, "Men are *cruel*, mean, rotten and savage."

When I leave for college, 90 miles west at the University of Massachusetts, I tell her I will write . . . and I do . . . but she does not reply. I tell college friends that I left a witch behind.

Fall semester, 1969: I am a first-year graduate student at the University of Michigan. In my postal box a letter from . . . Nancy. She tracked me down. Nancy had been packing up her old bedroom in Framingham where she found a condolence letter I sent when her Dad died in 1966. Now she wonders how I am doing.

How am I doing? That boy in high school, a mediocrity (and short, to boot), got his growth spurt in college and grew into a Big Man on Campus. This is before the invention of e-mail. We exchange two or three postal letters a week and make plans to spend New Year's Eve together in Boston.

As I wait to see Nancy, I think back five years to the madness of our courtship. Though it was torture not to ask about the past, I hold back because I am playing the long game. What if this is meant to be the Love of my Life? Would my obsession with the past wreck any possibility of a future together? So, I choose to speak only in the present tense. And I get the worst of both worlds. My desire to learn what our high school romance was all about is thwarted and, by the end of the week, I am bored, bored, bored with Nancy. I cannot wait to get back to Ann Arbor.

on the **Self-Help** shelf,
next to *Dating for Dummies*,
Dating Old Photographs
I put it back in **Antiques**
and move on to **Poetry**

141 | Proud Heart's Slave

Daniel Zender

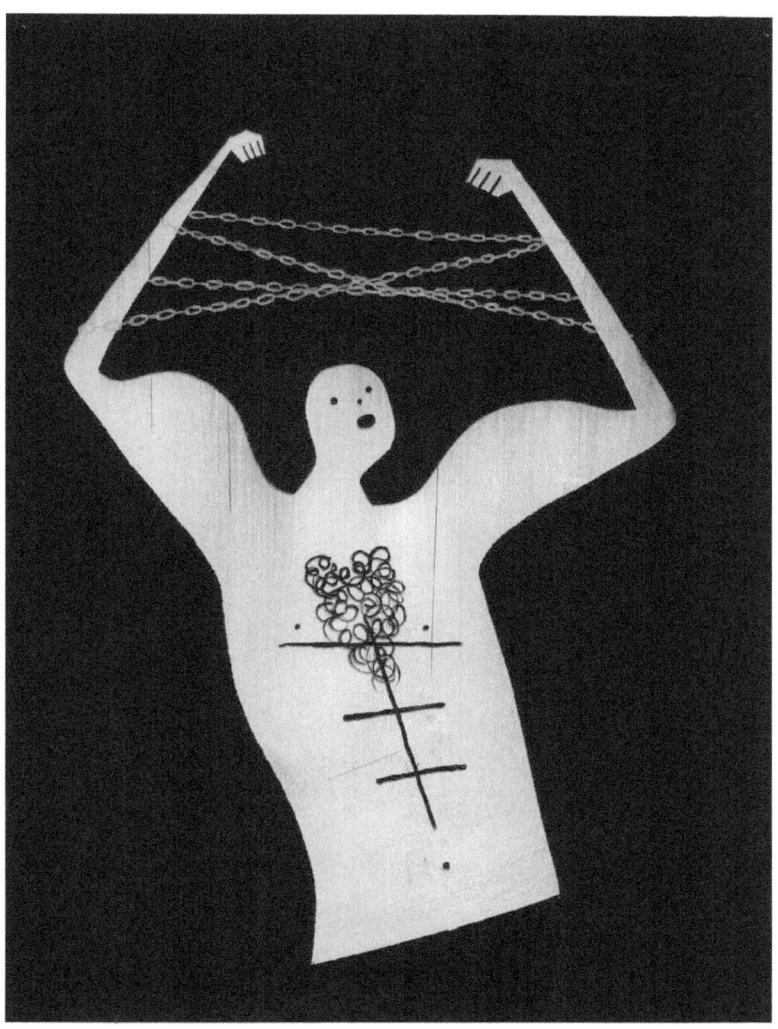

142 | Before the Tribulation

Maggie O'Connor

Come home and let's drink a spell.
Sort all this out. Church this morning—
actions all at once providing guilt.
And contradiction. Absolution. Pitchers
of dark & stormy wait for you on the porch.
Or perhaps the call for something stronger
to hold all this up. In the meantime, I think
I shall avoid God and the Holy Spirit; but
Jesus in Omaha haunts the small parts of me.
The space behind my ear. The crease below
by protruding hip bone. His promised return.

143 | Euphemism and Taxonomy: Wild Domestic Birds

Alexandra Edelblute

Each of your distractions is a gallus gallus domesticus.
Pastimes, quandaries, dalliances might as well
be Lakenvelders, Araucanas, Speckled Sussex: different

breeds of the same species. You and they
are entangled, are a tumble of
parts—hock, fluff, hackle—the wattle

and daub in a crude
wall I can't climb. You pass your time
with varicolored avian, the ornamental raised for show.
   Troubles

have tufty peduncle and missing backbone with prick-
sharp beaks to pinion you. Nighttime cockerels are willing
table-poultry, common and misled. People may say

you're callous, callous, frivolous, may read
thoughtless and naive, but I'm charmed as you chase your
untamed birds. I know how you are drawn

to their euphony, a carnival of wings quivering vibrato
like the chime of stirred pebbles in creek, the hypnosis
of their red-eyed interruptions. When you're

ready, when you're ready, when
the feathers have cleared the air and covered
the floor, and the talons rest in dirt, know

I've been behind you on the ground, now under
the down, not gallus gallus domesticus but nevertheless
a fowl, unhatched, waiting for your warmth.

144 | Ackuna's Bad Translator

Ross McCleary

Discouraged and helpless,
There are a lot of distractions:
Los Angeles, the last time.
Because of that
You will lose your wife.
On the right side of the angels,
Brain;
Consistent with the absence of meat,
Oh my God, this is not good.
To be honest, but this is controversial
However, here
Do you know? The difference in the world:
    Parliament is not very secure,
    Production of the old bad Angel has much better results.

145 | Re: CXLV

Andy Decker

:)

Wed, Jul 03
11:15am

>   Im late
>   ----------------------
>   Wed, Jul 03
>   11:20am

>   (O.O)
>   ----------------------
>   Wed, Jul 03
>   11:32am

>   *for school
>   ----------------------
>   Wed, Jul 03
>   11:32am

146 | When My Mother Calls Me Thin

Caroline Tanski

I snap, "I don't assign particular
value to thinness." All my life she has told me
beauty is equal parts health and kindness, so much
that I began to believe her. With age I find
vice closer tied with virtue: vanity calls
for self-deprivation. Yet there's no nutritional
value to guilt, no forgiveness found in a cupcake.
God won't care if I pluck my eyebrows each day;
my liver doesn't judge my Netflix queue.

We cannot be good all at once. A body
holds only so many merits, but contains
ample space for all faults. So leave me
to my minor sins, to my everyday sacred
imperfection. I try to find beauty
in clean, pink lungs, in books read and friends
kept. Still I primp and dress and maquillage.
The body has never been simple, and someone
in the end must feed all the worms.

147 | Weak Constitution

Lisa Ampleman

> My love is as a fever longing still
> For that which longer nurseth the disease.
> —*Sonnet 147*

You're the hectic in my blood,
the bacteria on my spoon,
the heated remnants of my appendix
curdling in my gut. But I despise

you. I ferret you out and lick
the bottom of your shoes—morsel
of a leaf, soil, salty rain—spit-shine them
clean. Like a raccoon

on trash night, with his little
people-hands, you can rummage
through my cans unimpeded.
I'll take the antitoxin, bubble-gum

flavored, and sweat you out
the next time, or the next.

148 | Mine Eye

Dianne Berg

Leave that thing alone!
One day you'll go blind.
Crap. My mom was right.

149 | Sinew is a Thing We Have Uses For

Chris Emslie

Point to a limb & call it pride. Watch me dismantle three walls & call it a world. This taking-down precedes loss, as in a fire. As in write me a catalogue, I'll rough out a prayer.

—

Pitch a mirror to the sky & be damned with false applause. What pleases the eye does not please the deer in the road, or the jaws in the rabbit. A tiny heart has been offered up. How it careens into myth. How god is a surgeon with a chainsaw. We are told every day to open our lives to something.

—

If there's a part of me that is not yours it's because I swallowed it. There's a thing people say about that which feeds but I have a literature for head, not the other way around. Is love more than obeisance when it's a boot to your temple?

—

Baby, at endgame no-one plays for keeps. That's the shitty thing about love: winter's easy. We wear success like a coat of muscle. Underneath it, we shrink.

150 | Still Life with Unrequited Love

Jennifer Franklin

I stitched my heart to him to heal his hurt.
But you are the only one who could ever
Love me—I feed your insatiable desire
For praise. Even after I saw the mean-spirited
Mind that lurked beneath the empathy
Of your written words, I still want you—
To rescue you from sorrow. I am satisfied
To feel your cruel love from across our
Wide river. But if you were here, you could
Turn this asylum into song, sung into my ear
To stay me. In my Gitto blue bedroom,
I can feel the way you would kiss
The scars on my neck as if they were sugar,

As if they were sonnets, as if they were stars.

151 | Conscious Young, Body Treason

Kevin Barton

152 | Here & Not Here: New Love Bearings

Jennifer Murvin

Here

My son Ethan came to the front door after the three days wearing clothes I did not buy for him. We said a quick goodbye to his father, my former husband. We did not watch him walk or drive away.

"Who bought those for you?" I asked Ethan about the shoes, which were Pumas. I asked him even though of course his dad had bought them. They were white and sleek and thin on his growing feet. They had velcro instead of laces. They were beautiful shoes. I had bought him three pairs not long before. Shoes from Target. He was five years old; he had scuffed them all in a week.

"Dad."

"I like your shirt," I said. White, with little red stripes across the front, a tank top, perfect for summer. He had new pants on, too, a bright orange. He would have not looked out of place in Cancun or south Florida or Whole Foods. He was a little boy going places. He had the look of a young man at a party who knows everyone, who makes a margarita with a secret ingredient as simple and brilliant as beer.

Every time he came home, there was an awareness of time passing, of time already passed. When I snuggled him at bedtime, he held me to his chest.

"We went to the mall," he said now. He was casual, making his way to the Legos.

"Oh," I said. I did not ask, did you get a cookie? A soft pretzel? Did someone hold your hand in the parking lot?

"You are so handsome," I said. He was a little different every time he came home from the three days away from me. His eyelashes were darker, like a Spanish woman's. He had new words: ridiculous, Mississippi, Titanic.

Not Here

On Sunday morning, I bring Ethan to his father's condominium to begin their three days together. This is the routine. I've been inside the fifteenth floor apartment, mostly in the early days of the divorce when the former husband and I thought we could be friends, better friends even. We didn't have to lose anything. One of the rooms in the condo has a wall entirely made of mirrors. This room is where he has put the pool table, which we bought while I was pregnant with our son, thinking it might be a thing to do during the nights home with a new baby. We had sex on it only once. In college, I had taught him how to play nine ball, to use the stick to imagine angles for a ricochet. The condo has three bedrooms and two balconies, which star in my nightmares: Ethan wanders outside, unsupervised, and somehow climbs the chair to look at the view. The nightmares stop there, him peering over, fifteen floors up, maybe a bird or snow, a feeling of horror. The hallways are carpeted and smell like spices or wet towels or old cologne, carpet that has known a lot of cooking but cooking not performed by the same person. The doormen are both in their seventies. One told Ethan he had been in the air force and that he loved the feeling of flying, like a superpower. He imagined Ethan might like comics. In Springfield, Missouri, the Ozarks, all hills and churches and small restaurants and trucks and phrases such as, "I am tickled to see you," or, "What time to you get home of an evening?", Ethan rides an elevator up to his condo and has a thirty-four inch flat screen television in his own room. His room's large windows overlook the city's regional baseball field, and on the rare Friday night he is at his father's condo, Ethan can watch fireworks explode below.

Here

The grocery store is the scene of our showdowns. There could be whistling, a tumbleweed. I could be wearing a long coat that dusts the road. Ethan could be approaching, hand to hip, his father's eyes framed in my mother's lashes, narrowed.

"Can I play on your phone?" No. When he has my phone he bumps into the cart, wanders like a drunk man.

"Can I sit in the cart?" No. He is far too tall, too big now, almost six years old. When he sits in the cart, in the little front section where he faces me, his legs get stuck, his shoes bent in odd angles, my purse hanging awkwardly from my shoulder, full of books, my students' paragraphs waiting to be graded.

"This is the worst day!" he says, small fists thumping against his thighs. This woman smiles, that woman frowns, that man examines a pineapple. "Why do you always take me to the store? Why do I have to go to the store? Why can't you go without me? I never have to go to the store with my dad! I want my dad! Why am I with you so much? I'm with you for a hundred days!"

The butter is on sale. I might make cookies. I should take some to the neighbors like my mother would.

"Can I have a chocolate milk?" No. Too much sugar this close to dinner time.

He is so thirsty. He is so thirsty, he is going to die. I am going to let him die of thirst.

Pringles? No. Cookies? No. No no no. I grab his arm a little too tight and pull him toward the cart.

"You're hurting me!" The cart is squealing. "It's not fair! You don't let me stay with my dad! You have me for a hundred days!"

"I love having you. I'm lucky to have you."

"Stop bragging!" His voice carrying across the tomatoes.

Sugar-free pudding for his lunches this week. Almonds. I won't have time to shop after this, more snow is coming.

We could have chicken pasta tonight, spaghetti. I could splurge, make Chicken Marbella, the dish my childhood best friend's British mother cooked for birthdays and graduations before the colon cancer strangled her from the inside. Ethan loves the prunes, cooked in olive oil, garlic, oregano, capers, brown sugar, wine. I need the smell of it tonight, I decide. The memories it brings to me this far from where I grew up in California.

I have explained again and again. The cereal aisle my witness. His dad and I love him, we both want him, I get him four days, Dad gets three, I get weekends so it feels like more. He can call his dad any time, I didn't make the decision. I love having him with me, I feel lucky to have him, I always want him. His dad always wants him. No chocolate milk this close to dinnertime, no cookies before dinner. Fruity Pebbles are bad for him, I don't care if he gets them at Dad's, Mommy has Honey Nut O's. He will not die of thirst, suck it up, swallow your spit.

By the time we are in line, he is crying. I am the meanest Mom on earth, I never let him have anything. When he has children, he will give them whatever they want, all the time.

"Will that be it, ma'am?" The cashier does not look at me.

In the car, he wants to play on my phone.

"Absolutely not." In the quiet privacy of the car, I am able to raise my voice. I ask, How could he do this me? Embarrass me in the store like that?

He hates this! He hates the store! Why do I do this to him?

I say, He is pushing it, really pushing it. Does he want to lose his bedtime story?

No, no, he'll be good, he's just so tired, no recess today, again! It's so cold! They won't let him out for recess! He loves me!

I love him, I always love him, but he cannot keep doing this in the store!

He's sorry, Mommy. He is the worst!

He is not the worst. He is not the worst. I always love him. I would like the put the store behind us. Should we start over?

Yes, he's sorry for being naughty. He loves me. He wants to start over.

Great, good.

(Pause.)

Can he play on my phone?

Not Here

A week after living my new house, I discovered that when I filled up the bathtub, the power went out. Not just my power, but the power to the entire block. This happened often enough that I understood the two events were connected, like the moon and the tides. Turn on the hot; watch the lights flicker; listen to the airy electrical sound as the light bulbs burst dead; observe the sparks from the transformer in the backyard trees like a failed firework; walk naked over wood floors.

The water in the bath, in the dark, was lavender, warm, amniotic. In the bath, I observed my stomach, my thighs, my freckles, shaved bubbles from my legs in strips. Here, tiled walls made every move echo-worthy. Here, I made lists: milk, toilet paper, crayons, swing set. I read books with lines like, "There have been three presidents since I held her in my arms." This night, Ethan was at his dad's house, and so his room a door down the hall was empty. I had been in the house two weeks. I had begun to close

Ethan's door the nights he was not here. He was only four and did not know what it meant that his parents had divorced and he lived in two houses now. I did not know what it meant. What he did know: A boat will sink when filled with too many Legos. Water left inside the plastic whale makes it smell. What I knew: The lavender I grew in a pot on the step could be dried and combined with oils and Epsom salts in an airtight container and in my bath, its grains crunched pleasantly under my back. I could afford the mortgage for the new house on my own without the alimony but not without the child support.

The three nights a week my son was at his father's house, and I took long baths and too often, the power went out. I was not afraid of the dark, but dark water made me afraid.

My house and the houses around mine plunged into primal, historical night. My bathtub controlled the electricity of a block of houses in the small neighborhood just south of the university where I taught, blocks away from a Spanish professor, the English Education professor, houses with dogs and children and retired grandparents and gardens. Springfield, Missouri, home of my son's father, his father's mother and father and sister and brother, birthplace of Brad Pitt, headquarters of Bass Pro Fishing. My neighbors couldn't make sense of the power outages. On these nights, typically between the hours of 8 and 11 p.m., they might have to rush to their children, to their candles and flashlights. The television show was recording, hopefully, but what if it wasn't? They'd been waiting all week for the new *Mad Men*. This activity was because of me, my bathtub, the new-to-me house with the 1950s stove that pulled out from the oven like a secret room.

I didn't call the electrician for a long time.

Instead I thought about how my widowed aunt left a pair of man's shoes outside her front door to imply that a large, formidable man lived there, too.

I imagined what it would be like to call the electrician, to answer the door with my hair wet. What if I saw the electrician and I wanted him to put his hands on my hipbones? What if I wanted him to kiss me, fill me with his electrician smells of lightening and drywall dust? What if I asked him to please stay while I took a bath, please guard outside the door? Please come in, I am so lonely in the darkness.

In my mind the electrician comes to the door with one of those old Victorian lamps. His eyes are glowing orbs and his teeth are very white as he tells me how beautiful I look in candlelight, how he will fix everything that needs to be fixed, how everything is under control.

Here

October. Mums like jewelry on porch steps, leaves the color of amber beads, rust, dying coals. There is rain in the wind even when the sky is clear, rain coming from the leaves themselves.

Ethan's 6th birthday party will be at my house, will include my parents and pregnant sister flown in from California as guests, my best friends and their children, some new friends made in the few months Ethan has been in kindergarten. The former husband has called to insist on bringing his new girlfriend to the party. Cassie is twenty-one years old to my thirty-one, a fashion major at the university where I teach, and she is blond and petite and the opposite of myself in the way that I have dated men who are writers with no money and beautiful words and tortured childhoods.

I have met Cassie a few times; she is pretty, girlish. Her slightly crooked front teeth and high voice bring out motherly feelings. If she were my student, I would find her open face comforting, I would want to teach her something. She reminds me of a babysitter, old enough to drive a car, young enough to make this barter because every night for her can be a weekend night. She is, in fact, the perfect person for the former husband: grateful, sweet. She is kind to Ethan, plays with him, takes photographs. She smiles at me when I see her and is eager to chat if I ask her a question.

But I say no, she can't come. I tell him, Fuck. You. It is the period of time after the divorce when I speak to the former husband primarily in curse words.

He says it was my choice to have the party at my house, I could have had it at a neutral location, and I say, like last year in that fucking shithole?

"Yes, like last year at Incredible Pizza," he says.

I do not say, I want a party for Ethan like the parties we had before the divorce, parties at our home where I have planned crafts and gift bags and cooked pots of chili and baked loaves of pumpkin bread. The phrase lands softly in my mind: a family party.

"Fuck you fuck you fuck fuck you," I say, because my life right now is the redefinition of the word family and that work is exhausting me, especially when my only language is curse words.

Of course, Cassie will come to the party.

The morning of the party, I imagine Cassie in my bathroom, her eyes over my soap, my perfume the former husband might recognize from the twelve years that came before her, the years she was ages nine through twenty-one.

In the hour before the party begins, I leave to pick up cupcakes and choose this time to call and inform my former husband of his half of the party bill.

"Do you have receipts?" he says.

"Asshole."

"It's not that I think you would lie about the amount, I just want to know what the money's going to," he says. He is very rich. He makes ten times the salary I earn as a college instructor.

"No. Fuck you."

"You can't call me the hour before my son's party and tell me I need to bring a check!" he yells.

Why have I called? I have no idea. It's our son's party. I paid for the cupcakes and the woman at the bakery had been kind, worn a scarf on her head and flour on her hands. My parents are looking at me like I have been diagnosed with a terminal disease. My father has noticed two kinds of wood in my floors. My sister's belly is beautiful with my niece growing inside.

When I arrive at home with the cupcakes, my mother recognizes the look on my face and removes the boxes from my arms. The cupcakes are red velvet, lemon, pumpkin, chocolate, sweet cream, some with little candies on top in corresponding flavors and shapes. I tell her, I want the party to be perfect. I tell her about the fight, and I can see her shoulders actually, physically square up. She will protect Ethan, myself, from this emotion she sees in my face. To call it anger would be too narrow, to call it grief would be closer, but I am not jealous of the new girlfriend. The emotion is Ethan turning six years old, those years passing like waking up in the dark. The emotion is his large white shoes, the memory of fall afternoons as he kicked me from the inside, kicked me all the way out. The emotion is my new house where I have painted the walls a soft pale green, the rooms clean and open and vulnerable. My parents' casual, fundamental partnership. I do not know enough ways to curse.

Ethan never stops smiling during the party. He is swinging on the new swing set, my birthday present for him, with his friends. He is swinging into the sky. He is pretending to be a pirate and there are enough children for a thorough pretending. Soon he is eating pizza, eyeing the presents piled up on the piano. He is eating a pumpkin cupcake, he is shining as a room of thirty people who love him sing Happy Birthday. I breathe. My closest girlfriends flock around me in protective detail. One, I notice, is posted to the kitchen, another outside. I have lit a fire in a fire pit installed days after Ethan drew a picture in school of his "Favorite Things," which featured a mother and son roasting marshmallows. Former husband and Cassie remain at a careful distance from me. They chat with my neighbor. I see my former husband's sister touch my sister's pregnant stomach.

Everything is fine. Most of this is love.

After the kids assemble construction paper and small puffy balls in the shape of turkeys, we go outside for the piñata. It is shaped like a spaceship.

Somehow the children are lined up and I have taken on the task of wrapping handkerchiefs around their heads and the former husband is supervising the spinning and the hitting. We move in a sort of tandem, circling children through the line, wrap the head, hand over the bat, moderate the swinging. He and I fall into rhythm, both taking the lead in this final activity at our son's birthday party.

My parents and my sister and the friends who knew us when we were married watch this. I watch it myself, the two people whose son was born to them six years ago, this man and woman who used to share a home, a bed, a life, a name. But there is no more shock or sadness.

Like driving by a house you had lived in once. The emotion is the new paint, the uprooted tree. And you drive on.

Not Here

How does the mother sleep in a house while her child's bedroom is empty? Is she even a mother in those times, or something else? What would that something else be? When he is not there, she cleans his toys, washes his laundry, reaches across his cartoon yogurts toward the wine. She does it because this is the life she has chosen.

Did she choose this? It seems melodramatic to say it was this or die. Even that is a lie. The only way she could choose this life is that she had no idea how it would feel to sleep in a house where her child's bedroom is empty. She understood this only after she had decided, which was the only way she could have decided, in the fog of that ignorance. But she cannot undo the awareness any more than she can undo this new life.

"Are you happy now?" the former husband asks her.

Hope is itself a form of happiness.

The mother has a job teaching creative writing at the university. She writes comments on her students' stories such as, "Is this ending too tidy?" She reads their stories about cancer patients, grandparents with dementia, zombie lovers, neglected children, abusive husbands, cheating wives, serial killers, trees that talk, detectives who are the criminals, landscapes, the first hunt, the first kiss. She corrects commas, throws names of stories and writers out to them like confetti. Her former students visit her with new stories for her to read. They lend each other books and she feels in these moments not completely emptied.

She meets her friends for breakfast crepes and baked cinnamon apples, laughs and discusses their children and love lives and divorces and new jobs. Sometimes she reads the women lines from her new essays and they listen for the parts where they are the characters. She calls her pregnant sister and helps plan the baby's going home from the hospital outfit, white with pink bows, a pink headband from Etsy, white booties. She orders her pregnant sister a necklace with the new baby's name on it, the baby's birthstone. She books flights. She cooks small dinners and doesn't do the dishes until the next day. She meets friends at 8 p.m. at a local wine bar that makes its own coffee. Her baths are made of lavender and books and the dog who won't stop licking her shoulder.

Her bedtimes are made of setting the house alarm and checking email and dreaming about men she has known and not known, their hands and mouths, the weight of their bodies, and sometimes the imagining is enough but mostly it is not.

In all of these hours, she is wondering if her boy is safe and if he is happy. What he is eating for lunch. Does he have his gloves? He would love this song. Did he turn in the form to his teacher? Did the former husband remember to bring snack? Is her boy brushing his teeth? Is he in bed now? Is he up yet? What were his dreams? Does he remember her. Will he come back.

When he is here, her parenting is in gesture—her body as mother, the physical business of loving and caring for a child. He climbs her, pulls on her hair, pokes her face, refuses to put on his shoes, takes off his socks because the seam feels wrong. She moves the hair from his forehead, rubs his back, flips his eggs, heats milk for cocoa, tends his dishes. She absorbs his accusations, his refusals, his resistance, his deep and trusting love. He tests, she explodes, he cries, she cries. She makes choices and she instructs, apologizes and makes mistakes and learns and makes mistakes and feels radiant and guilty and defeated and there is nothing, nothing like this love.

This is the work. His fingers run along her arm as she reads the words of his books. He takes her pillow, sleeps with his feet against her chest, breathes little boy breath into her face. Her home is an extension of her body, her body being his first home. The curtains over his windows, the quilt chosen for its warmth in weight and color, photographs of the faces of the people cast into and out of his life. The choice and the action and mess of Legos and airplanes and puzzles and superheroes and books and his endless art, his jeans and shirts and sweaters and jackets and socks and shoes. Her body is tired at the end of these days, she sleeps hard if not dreamless after the work of her mothering.

When he is not here, she must turn all of this inward. Maybe not unlike how it was when she carried him within her, when parenting was simply and not simply an awareness of him, a fundamental rooting from which he is free now. It was an utterly intimate, private change, a rewiring. When he is not here, the mothering turned inward overwhelms everything else. This does not stop her from teaching, writing, cooking, eating, cleaning, walking the dog, kissing an artist, planting her roses. It does not stop as the rivers do not stop even as they are being shaped by the earth. It does not stop as the wind does not stop even as it is funneled through trees and hair, as the words in a book do not stop haunting the reader until she can come home, unfold the page, take up the story.

153 | Sonnet 153 while you were sleeping

Pamela Allen Brown

The moon tucks her red nose under a black quilt
patched with grapes.

The ghost of a duck sleeps at her thin feet.

> *Cupid laid by his brand and fell asleep*
> *In a cold valley-fountain of that ground*

When she wakes her feet turn to stars.
Her yellow pencil draws fresh stars on blue cloth.

> *I sick withal the help of bath desired*
> *And thither hied . . .*

She floats through mud without getting her feet dirty.
She turns sad woods to thick fur, lit by silver candles.

> *A dateless lively heat still to endure*

Her duck wakes and quacks out dreams.
She sweeps bad ones into the closet and closes it tight.

> *against strange maladies a sovereign cure*

Hunting noises she pulls them off,
like a hairy blanket that itches.

Naked, happy, she looks in the pond and preens.

154 | I Don't Understand Shakespeare's Sonnet #154

Wayne Koestenbaum

I don't know who the love-god is or why he's asleep. I don't know why a branding-iron inflames his heart. I don't know why chaste nymphs shop for keepsakes and then throw their souvenirs in the Thames. I don't know why, ransacking a shtetl closet, I found cocaine in a mink coat's pocket (as if the laden article were a relic from an Isaac Bashevis Singer story I'd misremembered). I don't know why the pianist lit a votive candle: to aid her seduction of my chaste worthless body in the mountain chalet? I don't know why Dad came down with Legionnaires' Disease and re-proposed to Mom, though she'd long ago exiled him and pronounced him false. I don't know why Buster Keaton (my nickname) desires no one, only a cocktail sign neon-lit in the Nevada desert. I don't know why virgins keep their virginity, or why ephebe butts are considered cute near graduation-time, or why it is the responsibility of bucktoothed coloraturas to apostrophize a novice rear's rotundity. I don't know why the painter put her prosthetic arm on the seminar table and then asked a pert question about blindness, or why I sang "Suicidio!" offpitch as substitute for vespers. I don't know why my Sunday School teacher Mrs. Forkash was prettier than the previous year's Sunday School teacher, or why minor differences in prettiness are solemn as state secrets. I don't know why taking a bath with my brother provoked no hard-on, at least not a hard-on I can remember, and I remember every hard-on, especially the kitsch ones, the nepenthe ones, the hard-ons that have the power (even in retrospect) to eviscerate my will to survive. I don't know why after kissing the diseased man my lips felt tingly and chapped, as if I'd covered them with Tabasco sauce. I don't know why the sick man allegedly found his trick in the library basement, and why I imagined that the death-bringing trick was well-hung. I don't know why smallpox on blankets creates genocide, but I know a genocide when I see one, and I'm the poet here; I'm the loser who gets to decide how the poem ends.

Afterword | Remixing as Performance

Ayanna Thompson

Remixing Shakespeare's sonnets is nothing new. Shakespeare's plaintive concerns about his mortality have provided a type of clarion call that resounds over the centuries to writers who seek to fulfill his desire for increase and immortality. Stephen Greenblatt, for instance, famously voiced his "desire to speak with the dead" (1) at the beginning of *Shakespearean Negotiations*, and he ultimately acknowledged that his communion with Shakespeare had to be communal: "If I wanted to hear one [voice], I had to hear the many voices of the dead" (20). Although couched in a metaphor, Greenblatt's claims became oddly literalized by many—as if he could actually hear the stories of the formerly living (the scholar as Ouija board phenomenon).

The poems in this special edition, however, offer something entirely different. They are a performance piece that works to create a queer community with Shakespeare at its center, but their Shakespeare remains fully dead and voiceless. Nonetheless, the poems' performances of queer desire imagine and create a Shakespeare as he might have been had he lived today. Remixing, then, releases the past (even the desire to experience the past, or "to speak with the dead") in order to experience the present more fully, vibrantly, and complexly.

I call this set of meditations a performance piece because the collection is so self-conscious of the fact that the act of writing and reading a sonnet sequence is a restored behavior. As Richard Schechner explains, "Performance in the restored behavior sense means never for the first time, always for the second to nth time: twice behaved-behavior" (36). Shakespeare's sonnets, of course, were riffing on a set of tropes and behaviors that were well known by his early modern readers—his alterations to the tropes are both startling and enjoyable precisely because the tropes are known. The meanings of any performance, of course, "need to be decoded by those in the know" (35), and this collection, like Shakespeare's sonnets, epitomizes actions, interactions, and relations that are restored, remixed, and re-presented.

The remixing in this collection engenders a distinct queer aesthetics that work against the notion that increase and immortality must be achieved through procreation and progeny. Like Stephen Guy-Bray's brilliant book, *Against Reproduction*, these meditations challenge the common trope of author as parent and text as child. The eyes that emanate from "self-love" (Shakespeare's Sonnet 3), for instance, are not ones that are haunted by fears of loss or the lack of offspring. On the contrary, they smolder with a desire that seems to transcend both the need for time and the need for partners.

Likewise, José Muñoz's queer aesthetics, as espoused in *Cruising Utopia*, seem to be at play in the asynchronic love triangles that are enabled in poems like "The Paul Simon Annotations, or, You Can Call Me Sonnet 110." Paul Simon, William Shakespeare, and Ari Friedlander commune together without the pressures and limitations of time, place, space, or social hierarchies. Queer utopias, after all, work against the strict linearity of progression from the genius/author/original to the fan/rewriter/sequel. In fact, it is made very clear in "When My Mother Calls Me Thin (146)" that even death provides a moment for a ménage-a-trios. For when Caroline Tanski writes, "The body has never been simple, and someone / in the end must feed all the worms," the reader can imagine Polonius, Hamlet, and Tanski enjoying a terrific, if surprising, sixth act to *Hamlet*.

Remixing, by its very name, assumes that a queer blending already always exists (the mix). One is simply mixing anew what was already mixed up before; there is never an a priori moment in mixing. Moreover, the performative elements of remixing are explicitly queered when William Shakespeare's puns on *will* expand and explode. "He" (Will) can *fuck, fill, press, piss, lick,* and*come* (just some of the verbs in "My Name is Will [136]") because "you" (the reader), "I" (the author), and "He" are satisfied (and satisfiable) participants:

> our wills fulfilled
> in this sequence
> of threesomes—me the third,
> the number reckoned none.

The performative elements of remixing are clearest when the reader understands her/his role in the process. We are never passive bystanders, even when we gaze back at the fenced-in, self-loving boy in "self-love," because we are constantly implicated in the mixing process, which in essence is Richard Schechner's definition of performance as "twice behaved behavior." So, gentle reader, go back to the beginning, pick up the blender, and enjoy cruising the remixed utopia of Shakespeare's sonnets.

Works Cited

Greenblatt, Stephen. *Shakespearean Negotiations: The Circulation of Social Energy in Renaissance England.* Berkeley: The University of California Press, 1988.

Guy-Bray, Stephen. *Against Reproduction: Where Renaissance Texts Come From.* Toronto: the University of Toronto Press, 2009.

Muñoz, José. *Cruising Utopia: The Then and There of Queer Futurity.* New York: NYU Press, 2009.

Schechner, Richard. *Performance Studies: An Introduction.* Third Edition. London and New York: Routledge, 2013.

Contributors

(Ordered by Sonnet Number)

Ayanna Thompson is a Professor of English at The George Washington University and Trustee of the Shakespeare Association of America. Her books include *Passing Strange: Shakespeare, Race, and Contemporary America* (Oxford University Press, 2011); *Performing Race and Torture on the Early Modern Stage* (Routledge, 2008); and *Colorblind Shakespeare: New Perspectives on Race and Performance* (Routledge, 2006). She is currently working on a co-authored book about teaching Shakespeare that is tentatively called *Shakespeare on Purpose*; a single-authored book on Shakespeare and revenge; and the introduction to the new Arden *Othello*.

1: Jordan Alexander Stein missed all the Shakespeare questions on the GRE. He teaches in the English department at Fordham University and tweets @steinjordan.

2: Anna Maria Hong is the Visiting Creative Writer at Ursinus College and was the 2010-11 Bunting Fellow in Poetry at the Radcliffe Institute for Advanced Study. The recipient of *Poetry* magazine's 2013 Frederick Bock Prize, she has recently published poems in venues such as *Boston Review, Green Mountains Review, Fence, Drunken Boat, Fairy Tale Review, Unsplendid, Beloit Poetry Journal, Southwest Review, 250 Poems: A Portable Anthology, The Volta, Verse Daily, POOL, Best New Poets,* and *The Best American Poetry.* She has received residencies from Yaddo, Djerassi, Kunstnarhusset Messen, and Fundación Valparaiso, and teaches poetry writing at the UCLA Extension Writers' Program.

3: Adam W. Clifton is a photographer from Eastern North Carolina, specializing in portraiture and storytelling.

4: Claudia Gary writes, edits, sings, and composes (tonally) near Washington DC. A 2014 finalist for the Howard Nemerov Sonnet Award, 2013 semifinalist for the Anthony Hecht Poetry Prize, and Pushcart Prize nominee, she is author of *Humor Me* (David Robert Books 2006) and several chapbooks. Her poems appear in anthologies such as *Forgetting Home* (Barefoot Muse Press 2013) and *Villanelles* (Everyman Press 2012), as well as in journals published in the USA, UK, Canada, and Amsterdam. She also writes articles on health for *The VVA Veteran, VFW,* and other magazines. In 2014 she will offer poetry workshops through The Writer's Center. Brave souls can hear some of Claudia's other music, including a vocal/instrumental trio setting of Shakespeare's Sonnet 18 and settings of several contemporary poems, in rough recordings on her two YouTube channels: "cygneify" and "cygneify1." She suggests you try to ignore the visuals that accompany them.

5: Jane Hoogestraat's book of poems *Border States* won the 2013 John Ciardi Prize and will be published by BkMk Press in 2014. In addition, she has published in such journals as *Elder Mountain, Fourth River, Image, Midwestern Gothic, Poetry, Potomac Review,* and *Southern Review.* She teaches at Missouri State University.

6: Stuart Barnes's poetry has appeared widely in publications such as *Assaracus, Cordite Poetry Review, Going Down Swinging, Mascara Literary Review,* and *The Warwick Review.* He is poetry editor of *Tincture Journal,* poetry reader for *Verity La,* and poetry / flash reader for *One Throne Magazine.* Recently, he completed his first full-length manuscript, *Blacking Out and other poems.* He tweets @StuartABarnes.

7: Ed Madden is an associate professor of English and director of Women's and Gender Studies at the University of South Carolina. He is author of three books of poetry: *Signals,* which won the SC Poetry Book Prize; *Prodigal: Variations*; and *Nest.* His poems appear in *Best New Poets 2007, The Book of Irish American Poetry,* and *Collective Brightness.* He is also the author of the chapbook *My Father's House,* a sequence of poems based on the time he spent helping with his dying father's home hospice care.

8: Stephen S. Mills is the author of the Lambda Award winning book *He Do the Gay Man in Different Voices* (Sibling Rivalry Press, 2012). He earned his MFA from Florida State University. His work has appeared in *The Antioch Review, PANK, The New York Quarterly, The Los Angeles Review, Knockout, Assaracus, The Rumpus,* and others. He is also the winner of the 2008 Gival Press Oscar Wilde Poetry Award. His second poetry collection, *A History of the Unmarried*(Sibling Rivalry Press) releases in September of 2014. He lives in New York City and can be found at stephensmills.com.

9: Seth Pennington grew up in the minnow farm capital of Lonoke, Arkansas, as the son of a mortician. He is the Associate Editor of Sibling

Rivalry Press and the poetry journal *Assaracus*. He served as Poetry Editor of *Equinox*, the student-run journal of literature and art at the University of Arkansas at Little Rock from 2012-2013.

10: Sonja Johanson currently serves as the training coordinator for the Massachusetts Master Gardener Association. She has had recent work appearing in the *Albatross, Dandelion Farm,* and*Shot Glass Poetry,* and was a participating poet in the Found Poetry Review's 2013 Pulitzer Remix Project. Sonja divides her time between work in Massachusetts and her home in the mountains of western Maine.

11: Verna Kale is a Visiting Assistant Professor in Rhetoric at Hampden-Sydney College. Her teaching and research interests include American literature, life writing, and gender studies, and she is currently at work on a biography of Ernest Hemingway.

12: Douglas Luman is currently braving the wilds of the Ozarks while pursuing his MFA at the University of Central Arkansas. He is also the Book Reviews editor for the *Found Poetry Review.*

13: Ivy Alvarez's second poetry collection is *Disturbance* (UK: Seren Books, 2013). A recipient of writing fellowships from MacDowell Colony, Hawthornden Castle and Fundacion Valparaiso, her work appears in journals and anthologies in many countries and online, including *Sou'Wester,Prairie Schooner* and *Best Australian Poems* (2013), with selected poems translated into Russian, Spanish, Japanese and Korean. Find her online at ivyalvarez.com.

14: Leah Brennan received her MFA in Fiction from Chatham University, where her manuscript, "The Bulletproof Line," was a finalist for Best Thesis. She taught creative writing in the Allegheny County Jail through the Words Without Walls program and translated for Watching America, a website that publishes English versions of foreign news articles.

15: Michele Seminara is a poet and yoga teacher from Sydney. Her writing has appeared in publications such as *Bluepepper, Tincture Journal, Verity La,* and *PASH Capsule.* She blogs at micheleseminara.wordpress.com and is on Twitter @SeminaraMichele.

16: Peter LaBerge is a freshman at the University of Pennsylvania. His recent poetry and critical work appears in such publications as *The Louisville Review, DIAGRAM, The Newport Review,BOXCAR Poetry Review, Weave Magazine,* and *Hanging Loose,* among others. In the past, he has been named a two-time Scholastic Art & Writing Awards Gold Medalist for Poetry and a commended Foyle Young Poet of the Year. He grew up in southwestern Connecticut and currently serves as the Founder & Editor-in-Chief of *The Adroit Journal*.

17: Barbra Nightingale has six chapbooks and two books of poetry, and has had over 200 poems published in journals and anthologies. She is a professor of English at Broward College, Ft. Lauderdale. Carol Todaro illustrated her poem.

18: Susan Grimm's poems have appeared in *Blackbird*, *Poetry East*, *The Journal*, and other publications. Her book of poems, *Lake Erie Blue*, was published by BkMk Press in 2004. She also edited *Ordering the Storm: How to Put Together a Book of Poems* (2006). She won the inaugural *Copper Nickel* Poetry Prize (2010) and the Hayden Carruth Poetry Prize (2011). Her chapbook *Roughed Up by the Sun's Mothering Tongue* was published by Finishing Line Press in 2011. She blogs at *The White Space Inside the Poem*.

19: Patrick Thomas Henry holds an MFA in Creative Writing from Rutgers University and is currently pursuing his PhD at the George Washington University. His fiction has appeared in *Lowestoft Chronicle*, *The Siren*, *Green Briar Review*, *Revolution House*, *The Writing Disorder*, *The Writing Disorder Anthology*, and *Northville Review*. He has also contributed reviews to *Necessary Fiction*, *Sugar House Review*, and *Modern Language Studies*. He lives in Alexandria, VA, with his fiancée and their cat.

20: A.W. Strouse is a poet who studies medieval literature in the English doctoral program at the CUNY Graduate Center. His poems, stories, and essays have appeared in various publications, and his book *My Gay Middle Ages* is forthcoming from Punctum. He co- operates and curates the Ferro Strouse Gallery. (awstrouse.com, ferrostrouse.com)

21: Haley Searls is a sophomore at The Ohio State University, majoring in Political Science and minoring in French. She also enjoys taking English classes, specifically creative writing, and writing poetry. After she graduates she intends on moving back to Washington D.C., where her parents reside, to attend law school.

22: Cameron Hunt McNabb is Assistant Professor of English at Southeastern University. She specializes in medieval and early modern drama and has publications in or forthcoming in *Neophilologus, The Shakespeare Bulletin, Pedagogy,* and *Early Theatre.*

23: Randall Mann is the author of three poetry collections: *Straight Razor* (where this poem also appears), *Breakfast with Thom Gunn,* and *Complaint in the Garden*. His poems and prose have appeared in *The Kenyon Review, The Paris Review, Poetry, Salmagundi,* and *The Washington Post.* He lives in San Francisco.

24: Ellen McGrath Smith teaches at the University of Pittsburgh. Poems have appeared in *Cimarron, Bayou, Quiddity, Sententia, The American Poetry Review,* and others. Her work has been recognized with an AROHO Orlando Prize, an Academy of American Poets award, a Rainmaker Award from *Zone 3* magazine, and a 2007 Individual Artist grant from the Pennsylvania Council on the Arts. A chapbook of her poems, *Scatter, Feed,* will be published this year by Seven Kitchens Press.

25: Born in Bloody Harlan, Kentucky, Rachel Danielle Peterson teaches on the island of Saipan. A poem from her manuscript is featured in *Literary Imagination.* More poems can be found in *Arsenic Lobster, Midwestern Gothic, Her Royal Majesty,* and *The Los Angeles Review.* "Elegy of the Gun," published by *LAR,* was just nominated for *Best New Poets,* and *Cleft of Sky,* was chosen as a Semi-finalist for the Trio Award for For First/Second Book by Trio House Press.

26: Michael D. Snediker is the author of *The Apartment of Tragic Appliances: Poems* (Punctum Books, 2013), *Queer Optimism: Lyric Personhood and Other Felicitous Persuasions* (Minnesota, 2007), and *Contingent Figure: Aesthetic Duress from Nathaniel Hawthorne to Eve Kosofsky Sedgwick* (under contract, Minnesota). He is Associate Professor of English at the University of Houston.

27: Maia Gil'Adi is an English PhD student at the George Washington University. Her research is in late 20th century and contemporary Latino Studies and Literature, focusing on notions of spectrality, monstrosity and haunting.

28: Krystal Marsh is a writer based in Philadelphia. She recently graduated with her MA in Shakespeare Studies from King's College London.

29: Jason Roush is the author of four books of poems: *After Hours, Breezeway, Crosstown,* and *Dispossession.* He teaches at Emerson College and New England Institute of Art.

30: Robert Whitehead received his MFA from Washington University in St. Louis. His poems have appeared in *Assaracus, Gulf Coast,* and *Vinyl.* He lives in Brooklyn.

31: Michael Slattery is a graduate student in the MLA program with a focus in English studies at the University of South Florida St. Petersburg where he also received his Bachelor's degree in English in 2012. He is also an Admissions Officer for the office of Graduate Studies at USFSP. Michael is currently working toward a creative writing assignment as his final project, largely inspired by elements of human sexuality as depicted in Shakespeare's sonnets and plays.

32: Tanya Camp's undergraduate training is in art & design, and she is currently a graduate student at American University.

33: Andrea Janelle Dickens is originally from the Blue Ridge Mountains in Virginia and currently lives in Arizona, where she teaches in the Writing Programs at Arizona State University. Her work has won an award from *New South Journal* and has also been printed in *Caesura, streetcake* (UK), *Ruminate, The Wayfarer* and by Silver Birch Press. In her spare time, she is a ceramic artist, beekeeper and desert landscaper.

34: Ann Cefola is the author of *Face Painting in the Dark* (Dos Madres Press, 2014), *St. Agnes, Pink-Slipped* (Kattywompus Press, 2011), *Sugaring* (Dancing Girl Press, 2007) and translator of *Hence, this cradle* (Seismicity Editions, 2007). She is also a recipient of the Witter Bynner Poetry Translation Residency from the Santa Fe Arts Institute and the Robert Penn Warren Award judged by John Ashbery.

35: Jeff Streeby holds an MFA in Poetry from Gerald Stern's program at New England College in New Hampshire. His poetry has appeared in *Ginosko, Southwest American Literature, Los Angeles Review, Rattle,* and many others. His poem "Biography" won the 2013 *Provincetown OuterMost Community Radio Poetry Award* judged by Marge Piercy. He is a Senior Lecturer in English and History at Assumption University in Bangkok, Thailand.

36: Talin Tahajian grew up near Boston. Her poetry has recently appeared or is forthcoming in *PANK, Word Riot, DIAGRAM, Hobart,*

Washington Square Review, and on *Verse Daily.* She currently serves as a poetry editor for *The Adroit Journal,* and she is an undergraduate student at the University of Cambridge, where she studies English literature and attempts to assimilate.

37: Alexandra Reisner is a writer based in New Orleans with roots in New York and, before that, Hungary. Her work has appeared in the *Carolina Quarterly, PANK, Cobalt Review, The Columbia Current,* and elsewhere. She loves words and their origins, but always has to stop and make sure in her head that she's about to say, "etymology," and not, "entomology," or is it the other way around? Find her on Twitter: @juvenalia.

38: Robert Darcy is Associate Professor of English at the University of Nebraska at Omaha where he teaches and studies early modern literature.

39: Lynn Schmeidler's poetry appears in *Drawn to Marvel: Poems from the Comic Books* (Minor Arcana Press), *Mischief, Caprice and Other Poetic Strategies* (Red Hen Press), *Room* and *Opium*magazines. Her chapbook, *Curiouser & Curiouser* won the 2013 Grayson Books Chapbook Contest. She teaches at the Hudson Valley Writers Center in Sleepy Hollow, NY.

40: Bryan Borland is founder and publisher of Sibling Rivalry Press and editor of *Assaracus: A Journal of Gay Poetry,* one of Library Journal's "Best New Magazines" of 2011. He is the author of the American Library Association-honored *My Life as Adam* and most recently of *Less Fortunate Pirates: Poems from the First Year Without My Father.* He lives in Alexander, Arkansas, with his husband, Seth Pennington. His website is bryanborland.com.

41: Lanette Cadle is an Associate Professor of English at Missouri State University, where she is also an editor for Moon City Press. She has previously published poetry in *Connecticut Review, Crab Orchard Review, NEAT,* and *Menacing Hedge,* and she has work forthcoming in *Elder Mountain.* She is a past recipient of the Merton Prize for Poetry of the Sacred.

42: Michael Flory, research scientist by day, quasi-Oulipian by night, is a regular at the Wednesday salons of that other noted W.S., the Writhing Society, a workshop devoted to the production of constrained writing.

43: Beth Gylys is a Professor of Creative Writing at Georgia State University. She has two published collections of poetry (*Bodies that Hum* and *Spot in the Dark*) and two chapbooks (*Balloon Heart* and *Matchbook*).

44: Zack Rosen's writing has been published in *The Washington Blade, Queerty, Out, The Advocate, The New Gay, Metro Weekly, Huffington Post, The New York Post, The Washington Post, Jezebel*, and elsewhere.

45: Edward Bevan lives in Putnam County New York, where he attempts to grow deer- and woodchuck-resistant gardens, and consistently fails. A graduate of Sarah Lawrence's MFA program in Poetry and Fiction, he works for a major IT company experimenting with new forms of employee engagement and education.

46: Jeffery Berg grew up in Six Mile, South Carolina, and Lynchburg, Virginia. He received an MFA from NYU. His poems have appeared in *Court Green*, the *Gay & Lesbian Review, Map Literary, Assaracus* and *Harpur Palate*. He has written reviews for *The Poetry Project Newsletter* and *Lambda Literary*. A Virginia Center of the Creative Arts fellow, Jeffery lives in New York and blogs at jdbrecords.blogspot.com.

47: Ana Garza G'z has an MFA from California State University, Fresno. Fifty of her poems have appeared in various journals and anthologies, most recently in *Damselfly* and *Pentimento*. She teaches and works as a community interpreter and translator.

48: Maria Schurr is a Pennsylvania native who now resides in Brooklyn. She first came to the city to study Creative Non-Fiction at The New School, where she received an MFA in 2008. Maria is a Library Technician at the Thomas J. Watson Library in the Metropolitan Museum of Art and volunteers as an Associate Editor for the heavily trafficked pop culture site PopMatters. Maria's work has appeared in *The Quay* and *Proteotypes*. She is a member of The Writhing Society, which champions constrained writing; her manipulations of Shakespeare's Sonnet 48 employ constraints practiced in the group. Maria likes dogs and her boyfriend. She also still likes New York.

49: Carol Dorf's poetry has been published in *Spillway, Sin Fronteras, Antiphon, Composite, Occupy SF, Fringe, About Place, The Journal of Humanistic Mathematics, Scientific American, Maintenant, OVS, Best of Indie New England Lit*, and elsewhere. Her chapbook, *Every Evening Deserves A Title*, is available from Delirious Nonce Publications. She is poetry editor of *Talking Writing* and teaches mathematics at Berkeley High School.

50: Bo McGuire hails from Hokes Bluff, Alabama. The son of a Waffle House cook and his third-shift waitress, he currently hammers out spectacles in the grad film program at NYU. He suffers the city mostly gladly. Other poems can be found in other places like *Handsome*, *Poets & Artists*, and *Lana Turner*. Palms up for Dolly Parton.

51: Kendra Leonard is a poet whose work has appeared in *Haggard* and *Halloo* and is forthcoming in *The Hartskill Review*.

52: Elizabeth Thompson received her M.A. in English Literature, with distinction, from George Washington University, where her research reflected on post-colonial liminal subjectivity and feminist geographies. She is the development communications manager for Institutional Advancement at Hood College in Frederick, MD. Born in Baton Rouge, Elizabeth's poetry borrows from rural aesthetics to examine urban political landscapes for queer women of color. She also enjoys cooking, and co-owns a small locally-sourced catering business, La Eats, with her husband. When she performs spoken word, Elizabeth's artist name is Ah-vek Mwa, a nod to her French Creole and West African roots.

53: Rita Cotera is a Latina disability rights activist and artist. Her work has been featured by *NPR, New York Times Magazine,* and *The Washington Post.*

54: RJ Gibson holds an MFA in Poetry from Warren Wilson College. He is the author of *Scavenge* (co-winner of the 2009 Robin Becker Prize) and *You Could Learn a Lot*. His work has appeared in *Court Green, Kenyon Review Online, The Cortland Review,* and in the anthologies *My Diva* and *Collective Brightness*. He is a Lecturer at West Virginia Wesleyan College.

55: Terry Belew is a creative writing student at Missouri State University. His poems have appeared or are forthcoming in *Poetry Quarterly, Midwestern Gothic*, and *Big River Poetry Review.*

56: Theodora Danylevich is a PhD Candidate in American Literature and Culture at The George Washington University. Academically, she writes about [sic]k performativity. Poetically, she dabbles in homophonic translation, of which some of her work with the Old English of Beowulf has appeared in *Vanitas 4, Phoebe,* and *DCPoetry.com.*

57: Bonnie S. Kaplan is a native Angeleno and a longtime teacher of adults in the California corrections system. She holds an MFA in Performance Art from the California College of Arts and Crafts. Her poems are published in *The Squaw Valley Review Poetry Anthology 2011*, *Adrienne Rich: A Tribute Anthology* (Split Oak Press, 2012), and *This Assignment is So Gay: LGBTIQ Poets on the Art of Teaching* (Sibling Rivalry Press, 2013).

58: Sylvia Sukop is a Los Angeles-area writer and photographer. She was awarded the PEN Emerging Voices Fellowship in 2009 and she has been a frequent contributor to *Flaunt*, *The Huffington Post*, and the photography journal *Exposure*. Her essay "Pioneers on the Frontier of Faith" will be published in an anthology exploring hidden histories of Los Angeles (forthcoming in 2015 from Heyday Press). Find more of her work at sylviasukop.com.

59: Gretchen E. Henderson has published two hybrid novels, *The House Enters the Street* and *Galerie de Difformité* (a book deforming across media), along with a collection of nonfiction, *On Marvellous Things Heard*, and a poetry chapbook, *Wreckage: By Land & By Sea*. Her cross-genre writings have been awarded the Madeleine Plonsker Prize and Mellon Postdoctoral Fellowship from MIT, and have appeared in a range of journals and anthologies, including *The Kenyon Review, The Iowa Review, Ploughshares, Black Warrior Review, Journal of Artists' Books*, and*The &NOW Awards: The Best Innovative Writing*.

60: Christopher Kempf is a Stegner Fellow in Poetry at Stanford University. His work has appeared recently in *Gulf Coast*, *The New Republic*, and *Prairie Schooner*, among other places. He currently lives in Oakland.

61: Sarah Grodzinski earned her MFA in Creative Writing from Chatham University. She is currently an Instructor of Writing at Lebanon Valley College. She has had poems published in *Off The Coast*, *The Burning Word Press*, and *The Red Clay Review*. When she is not writing, she enjoys playing tennis and going to concerts.

62: Aaron DeLee graduated with an MFA in Creative Writing from Northwestern University in 2013. He has been published in various journals, including *Court Green, Assaracus, Interrobang*, and others. He currently lives in Chicago, where he is training for his second "Tough Mudder."

63: Robert Adams, currently pursuing a BFA in Graphic Design at Missouri State University, has always been interested in the power of image. Using his training as a graphic designer, Robert produces a wide variety of visual art and illustration ranging from comics to commercial work. You can follow him at robatomic.tumblr.com.

64: Mario DiGangi is Professor of English at the City University of New York. His books include *Sexual Types: Embodiment, Agency, and Dramatic Character from Shakespeare to Shirley* (University of Pennsylvania Press, 2011) and *The Homoerotics of Early Modern Drama* (Cambridge University Press, 1997).

65: Donna Vorreyer is a Chicago-area writer who spends her days teaching middle school. Her work has appeared in many journals including *Rhino, Linebreak, Cider Press Review, Stirring, Sweet, wicked alice,* and *Weave*. Her fifth chapbook, *We Build Houses of Our Bodies*, is forthcoming this year from Dancing Girl Press; in addition, her first full-length poetry collection, *A House of Many Windows*, is now available from Sundress Publications. Vorreyer serves as a poetry editor for *Mixed Fruit* magazine. Visit her online at donnavorreyer.com.

66: Winston H. Plowes writes his words on a narrowboat on England's inland waterways. His compositions have been widely published, hopefully making people pause and ponder the magical details of life. Find Winston at winstonplowes.co.uk.

67: Natalie Byers has a MA in English from Missouri State University where she taught introductory poetry and worked on the editorial staff for the *Moon City Review*.

68: C. Russell Price received his BA from The University of Virginia and his MFA from Northwestern University. His work has appeared in *Assaracus, North Chicago Review, Weave,* and elsewhere. He currently serves as the Senior Poetry Editor of *TriQuarterly*.

69: A native of West Virginia, Kelly McQuain's writing has appeared in such venues as *Painted Bride Quarterly, Kestrel, Weave, The Pinch, Assaracus, The Harrington Gay Men's Fiction Quarterly,* and *American Writing*, as well as in numerous anthologies, including *Best Gay Erotica, Men on Men, Between: New Gay Poetry, Drawn to Marvel: Poems from the Comic Books, The Queer South* and *Skin & Ink*. His chapbook, *Velvet Rodeo*, recently won BLOOM magazine's poetry prize. He has worked as a comic book artist and a pretzel maker, but now works as a creative writing professor in Philadelphia. Visit him at kellymcquain.wordpress.com.

70: Christopher Crawford's poetry, essays and translations have appeared or are forthcoming in magazines like *The Rumpus, Plume, Rattle, The Collagist, Puerto del Sol, The Cortland Review, Weave* and elsewhere. He edits *B O D Y.*

71: Wendy Bashant was born in Seattle, attended Middlebury College, and received her Ph.D. in Victorian Literature at the University of Rochester. She has published poetry in various little magazines and scholarly articles in *The Pre-Raphaelite Journal* and *En Travesti: Opera and Gender Subversions.* She spent 15 years in Iowa, serving as chair of the English Department at Coe College, and 8 years in Florida at New College, the Honors College of Florida in Sarasota. Currently, she's at University of California, San Diego serving as the Dean of Students at Thurgood Marshall College.

72: Bjørn Palmqvist is a self-taught composer, musician and producer who's won several awards in Denmark. Worth mentioning are Statens Kunstfond's composer contest "Det hemmelige mærke" in 1999 and a sizable grant from the same Statens Kunstfond in 2001. His latest album from 2007,*Syng Hierte*, which was very well received by the critics, interprets psalms and poems by the Danish poet H.A. Brorson, sung by classical soprano Janne Solvang. Previous albums include*Reconstruct*, which critics named "a unique point of reference of its genre." Thomas Magnussen trained at the renowned drama school the Guildhall School of Music and Drama in London from 1997-2000. At the school he was taught the ways of classical theatre by some of the world's best teachers. He has among other things been part of the ensemble, which opened the Danish Royal Theatre's new playhouse in 2008, with a production of *Hamlet.* Together with friend and colleague Lars Mikkelsen he won the prestigious Danish theatre award "Aarets Reumert" in 2008 for the Shakespeare collage *Flammens Muse – Muse of Fire.* Two years later they were nominated again for yet another Shakespeare show: their all-male production of *Twelfth Night*, which marked the opening of the Copenhagen based theatre Republique.

73: David McAleavey's poetry has appeared in many journals, including *Ploughshares, Poetry,* and*The Georgia Review*; since early 2010 he has had over a hundred poems and prose poems in*Epoch, Poetry Northwest, Denver Quarterly, Birmingham Poetry Review, diode* *poetry journal,anderbo.com, Stand, Drunken Boat,* and dozens of others. His fifth and most recent book is *HUGE HAIKU* (Chax Press, 2005). He teaches literature and creative writing at The George Washington University.

74: Tom La Farge has written two novels, *Zuntig* and *The Crimson Bears*, and a book of tales, *Terror of Earth*. He co-founded the Writhing Society, a weekly salon for constrained writing in Brooklyn, and has published the first three pamphlets of a manual, *13 Writhing Machines*, explaining various constraints. He edits the blog writhingsociety.blogspot.com. "Three Writhings" appeared in the *&Now Awards 2009*. His cut-up chapbook *Life and Conversation of Animals* appeared in 2010. He's currently working on three novels in various stages of completion. He lives in Brooklyn and is Managing Editor of Proteotypes, the publishing arm of Proteus Gowanus.

75: Mark Ward is a poet, playwright, and noise musician from Dublin, Ireland. His plays include *The Middle Distance, Saliva,* and *Blue Boy*. He makes noise music under the name Where is This and runs the independent record label, Bored Bear Recordings. His prose has been published in *Jonathan* and the *Queer in Brighton* anthology. His poetry has been featured in *Assaracus, Glitterwolf, Storm Cellar,* and *The Good Men Project*. He has recently completed work on his first full-length collection, *Circumference*, which will form the first part of his *American G.I.* series. Find Mark at astintinyourspotlight.wordpress.com.

76: K. Tyler Christensen is a writer living in Washington, DC. His work has appeared in *Boise Weekly*, the *Tin House* blog — *Open Bar, The Rumpus*, and *The Huffington Post*. He is currently the Editor-in-Chief of *Folio*.

77: Pamela Johnson Parker is an instructor of creative writing and humanities at Murray State University. Her poems, short fiction, and essays have appeared in numerous journals anthologies, most recently *Language Lessons* from Third Man Press in Nashville. Parker lives in west Kentucky and is currently at work on a novel.

78: Michael Carosone is a writer, educator, and activist. He edited the book *Our Naked Lives: Essays from Gay Italian American Men* (Bordighera Press, May 2013), which is a collection of 15 personal essays on the lives of gay Italian-American men. His poems and essays have been published in a variety of books and journals. He writes on personal, political, and social issues, including marginalized peoples and literatures, especially the gay, lesbian, bisexual, transgender, and queer community. He is from Brooklyn and lives in Manhattan with his partner and dog.

79: Dr. Heather Ladd is an Assistant Professor of Restoration and Eighteenth-Century English literature at the University of Lethbridge in southern Alberta. She is currently working on comic representations of the book trade on the London stage.

80: Paul O'Brien is a Boston native and graduate of the Massachusetts College of Art and Design. He is currently the Studio Programs Coordinator at The Andy Warhol Museum in Pittsburgh, where he also leads the production of *Swishy*, a queer youth zine. Both his personal artwork and teaching practices center around queer portraiture.

81: Sara Button is an MFA candidate at the University of Pittsburgh. Her favorite supporting character in Shakespeare has always been Benvolio.

82: Grant Metzker is a portrait artist who teaches art on the Pine Ridge Indian Reservation in South Dakota.

83: Samuel R. Yates is a graduate student at The George Washington University, where he focuses on the adaptation of dis/abled human bodies from literature and film subjects into musical theater productions. As a dramaturg, playwright, and director, Sam has worked with the Abbey Theatre, The Eugene O'Neill Theatre Center, The Samuel Beckett Centre, and New Harmony Theatre, among others. Sam's previous plays include *Haunted*, *Beau*, and *grass greener*; his next project,*American, Other* will debut in Summer 2014.

84: Benjamin Steiner is a playwright with awards from the Los Angeles Playhouse, Wooly Mammoth Theater, and Chicago Fringe. He lives in Alaska with his partner.

85: Vincent James Trimboli is a native of Elkins, WV, and holds an MFA in Creative Writing from West Virginia Wesleyan's low-residency program. Vincent is a poet, actor, and visual artist; he currently teaches writing at Davis and Elkins College. Vince's essays and poems appear in *The Vandalia* and most recently in the second volume of Julianna Warner's *The Yesterday, Today and Tomorrow Project*.

86: Joshua Peter Kulseth holds a BA in English from Clemson University. He plans to pursue an MFA in creative writing next year.

87: Jonathan Hsy is Associate Professor at The George Washington University. He teaches and publishes on Middle English poetry, translation theory, and disability studies.

88: Christine Swint received an MFA in creative writing from Georgia State University in 2013, where she taught English composition and introductory poetry writing. A former Spanish instructor, she holds an MA in Spanish language and literature from Middlebury College and a BA in English and Spanish from the University of Georgia. Her poems have appeared most recently or are forthcoming in *Slant*, *Shadowbox*, *Flycatcher*, and *Tampa Review*. As a student, she won the 2012 Agnes Scott Writer's Festival Award in poetry.

89: Jack Kahn is a student and social media enthusiast from Claremont, CA. He writes about Twitter, race, digital media, viruses, disability, technoscience, narcissism, and celebrity.

90: Louis Maraj holds an MA in English/Creative Writing from Texas Tech and currently studies Renaissance poetics at The Ohio State University. His recent creative work can be found in *Spillway*, *New Texas*, *Rock & Sling* and is forthcoming in *Pea River Journal* and *Paper Nautilus*.

91: Jim Daniels' latest book of poems, *Birth Marks*, was published by BOA Editions in 2013 and was selected as a Michigan Notable Book. His next book of short fiction, *Eight Mile High*, will be published by Michigan State University Press in 2014. A native of Detroit, Daniels teaches at Carnegie Mellon University in Pittsburgh.

92: Wendy Walker's books include *The Secret Service*; *The Sea-Rabbit, or, The Artist of Life*, *Stories Out of Omarie*, *Blue Fire*, and *My Man and Other Critical Fictions*. She is a core collaborator at the Proteus Gowanus Interdisciplinary Gallery in Brooklyn, and the editor of Proteotypes, its publishing arm. With Tom La Farge, she leads The Writhing Society, a weekly salon/class devoted to the practice of constrained writing. Her work has appeared in *Conjunctions*, *3rd Bed*, *The Denver Quarterly*, *Parnassus: Poetry in Review*, *Chain*, *Open City*, *Mad Hatter's Review*, *The New Review*, *Exploring Fictions*, *Sentence*, and the anthology *I'll Drown My Book: Conceptual Writing by Women* (Les Figues). More at wendywalker.com.

93: Jessica Server earned her MFA in poetry and travel writing from Chatham University. She works as a teaching artist and writer in Pittsburgh, where she contributes a weekly food column for Pittsburgh City Paper. Her first chapbook, *Sever the Braid*, is currently available from Finishing Line Press.

94: Eléna Rivera's most recent books are *On the Nature of Position and Tone* (Field Press, 2012), *The Perforated Map* (Shearsman Books, 2011), and *Remembrance of Things Plastic* (LRL e-editions, 2010). She won the 2010 Robert Fagles Prize for her translation of Bernard Noël's *The Rest of the Voyage* (Graywolf Press, 2011) and is a recipient of a 2010 National Endowment for the Arts Literature Fellowship in Translation.

95: Dustin Brookshire is a poet & Dolly fanatic who calls Atlanta home. His debut chapbook, *To The One Who Raped Me*, was published in 2012 by Sibling Rivalry Press. Visit him online at dustinbrookshire.com.

96: Michael Walsh is the author of *The Dirt Riddles*, winner of the inaugural Miller Williams Prize in Poetry from the University of Arkansas Press as well as the 2011 Thom Gunn Award for Gay Poetry. His poetry chapbooks from Red Dragonfly Press include *Adam Walking the Garden* and *Sleepwalks*. He lives in Minneapolis.

97: Jay Stevenson is a photographer in New York City.

98: Julie Houchens is a third-year undergraduate Nursing student at The Ohio State University, and this is her very first literary publication. Her inspiration for her artwork occurred with the assignment of a sonnet remix project for her Introduction to Shakespeare lecture. She has a particular fondness for time well spent with friends and family, literature, and nature.

99: Sujata Iyengar teaches Shakespeare and English Renaissance Literature at the University of Georgia. With Christy Desmet, she co-founded and co-edits *Borrowers and Lenders: The Journal of Shakespeare and Appropriation*, the award-winning, online, scholarly, multimedia Shakespeare journal. Her last book, *Shakespeare's Medical Language*, was re-issued in paperback in April 2014.

100: Carlton D. Fisher is an Instructor in the English Department at SUNY Jefferson and a graduate student in the writing program at SUNY Binghamton. His work has appeared in *Assaracus, The Black*

River Review, The Paterson Literary Review, and is forthcoming in the spring 2014 issue of *Lips.* He is the author of the chapbook *Silhouette of a Man* and is currently completing work on a second chapbook, tentatively titled *Songs for the Empty Rooms,* which should be available before the end of 2014. He is a lifelong native of Northern New York.

101: Kelly Jones teaches college composition and works in a library. She has an MFA from the Creative Writing Workshop at the University of New Orleans.

102: Niamh J. O'Leary is an Assistant Professor of English at Xavier University in Cincinnati, OH, specializing in sixteenth and seventeenth-century drama. Her articles have appeared in *The Upstart Crow* and *The Shakespearean International Yearbook.* Her research focuses on representations of communities of women in Renaissance drama, particularly addressing issues of marriage, maternity, and ethnicity. She is currently writing about women in Shakespeare's Greek and Roman plays; organizing a conference in conjunction with a production of *The Two Noble Kinsmen*; and, with Christina Luckyj, co-editing a collection of essays on early modern women's political alliances.

103: RJ Ingram is an Ohioan who lives in Oakland, California. His cat Brenda lives in North Carolina and lost her leg while campaigning in the swing states. Upcoming work can be found in *Timber,Pinwheel,* and *Birdfeast.*

104: Based in Providence, Rhode Island, Beth Ayer is Senior Poetry Editor/Web Manager for the*Found Poetry Review.* Her work has been published in *Bukowski On Wry, Otis Nebula, Temper*and the *Silver Birch Press NOIR Erasure Poetry Anthology* (forthcoming). In April 2013, she was one of 85 poets to create poems from the 85 Pulitzer Prize-winning works of fiction as part of the*Pulitzer Remix* project. Find her at bethdayer.com.

105: Julian Modugno is a filmmaker and humorist residing in the plucky town of Atlanta, GA. His YouTube channel, Bland Hack Pictures, features numerous sketches about old comedy standbys like miscarriages, biracial identity issues, and the Brontë Sisters. His instagram features a pretty decent split between poorly-lit selfies, expertly-composed cat pics, and mind-blowing documentation of signage in the deep south, and can be followed on Instagram at @gafapasta. His entire ego is fueled by garnering "likes."

106: A book historian as well as literary scholar, Lindsay Ann Reid is a Lecturer in English at the National University of Ireland, Galway. Her research centres on late medieval and early modern England, particularly the Tudor reception of classical and medieval literary texts.

107: Kathy Gilbert lives in Daly City but usually can be found writing at the library at SFSU where she earned an MFA in Creative Writng (Poetry) in 2013. She retired from a 32-year career in public transit. She belongs to a dream group, too.

108: John J. Trause, the Director of Oradell Public Library, is the author of *Eye Candy for Andy (13 Most Beautiful . . . Poems for Andy Warhol's Screen Tests)* (Finishing Line Press, 2013); *Inside Out, Upside Down, and Round and Round* (Nirala Publications, 2012); the chapbook *Seriously Serial* (Poets Wear Prada, 2007; rev. ed. 2014); and *Latter-Day Litany* (Éditions élastiques, 1996), the latter staged Off Broadway. His translations, poetry, and visual work appear internationally in many journals and anthologies, including the artists' periodical *Crossings*, the Dada journal *Maintenant*, the journal *Offerta Speciale*, the Uphook Press anthologies *Hell Strung and Crooked* and *-gape-seed-*, and the Great Weather for Media anthology *It's Animal but Merciful*. He is a founder of the William Carlos Williams Poetry Cooperative in Rutherford, N. J., and the former host and curator of its monthly reading series.

109: Paul Strohm is a freelance journalist working in Houston, Texas. His poems have appeared in the*Berkeley Poets Cooperative, Green's Magazine, Deep Water Literary Journal* and other brave places.

110: Ari Friedlander is Assistant Professor of English at the University of Dayton. He has published essays in *SEL: Studies in English Literature: 1500-1900*; *Upstart: A Journal of English Renaissance Studies*; and *The Oxford Handbook of Shakespeare and Embodiment* (forthcoming 2014). His current book project, *Promiscuous Generation: Rogue Sexuality and Social Status in Early Modern England*, traces the literary figure of the rogue from a criminal to a more normative social register, exploring how rogue sexual liberty acted as a powerful solvent of social boundaries and helped produce early modern England as a profoundly unsettled socio-sexual world.

111: David B. Goldstein is the author of the poetry collection *Laws of Rest* (BookThug 2013) and a work of literary criticism, *Eating and Ethics in Shakespeare's England* (Cambridge UP 2013). He writes frequently on matters related to Shakespeare, early modern culture, and food studies, and his poetry and translations have been published in journals and anthologies across North America. David lives in Toronto with his wife, artist Mindy Stricke, and their two children. He is Associate Professor of English at York University.

112: Rachel Levens is a theater artist and recent graduate of Cornish College of the Arts (Seattle, WA). She works and lives in Brooklyn, NY and is an active member of the Writhing Society where she is practicing writing with constraints.

113: Poetry and essays by Brad Clompus have appeared in such places as *West Branch, The Journal, Poetry East, Willow Springs, Fifth Wednesday Journal, Zone 3, Tampa Review*, and *Sonora Review*. He is a humanities lecturer at Lesley University.

114: Kinsley Stocum is the founding poetry editor and web/layout designer for the fledgling online lit mag *IDK Magazine*. She graduated with her MFA in Poetry from Chatham University in 2014 and now spends most of her time on Instagram. Follow her on Twitter @kinsley17.

115: Randolph Pfaff is a poet, editor, and visual artist. His work has been featured in *PANK, The Destroyer, H_NGM_N, Revolver*, and *SLAB*, among others. He also edits a literary journal called apt and runs a small press called Aforementioned Productions. He's not very good at free time.

116: Cathleen Calbert's poetry and prose have appeared in many publications, including *Ms. Magazine,The New York Times*, and *The Paris Review*. She is the author of three books of poetry: *Lessons in Space* (University of Florida Press), *Bad Judgment* (Sarabande Books), and *Sleeping with a Famous Poet* (C.W. Books). She has been awarded *The Nation* Discovery Award, a Pushcart Prize, and the Mary Tucker Thorp Award from Rhode Island College, where she professes.

117: Martin Elwell is a New Hampshire based poet and editor. He is the author of the chapbook *Dreaming Again* (WPG Press). His poems have appeared in *Extract(s), The Found Poetry Review, Empty Mirror Magazine of the Arts* and other places. He co-edited *Bearers of Distance*, an anthology of poems by runners from Eastern Point Press, and he is News & Resources Editor for *The Found Poetry Review*. You can find him on Twitter @MartyElwell, read his poems at martinelwell.wordpress.com and follow his travels at wordspergallon.com.

118: Em Russell is a Philadelphia artist, trained at the Rhode Island School of Design, who focuses on street and performance art.

119: Alison Powell's first collection of poems, *On the Desire to Levitate*, will be published by Ohio University Press in March 2014. Her work has appeared in journals including *AGNI, Black Warrior Review, Boston Review, Crazyhorse, Guernica,* and others, and in anthologies including *Best New Poets 2006* . She is completing a PhD in English at the Graduate Center of the City University of New York.

120: Wythe Marschall is a writer and PhD candidate in the Department of the History of Science at Harvard University, where he studies twentieth and twenty-first century life sciences. His work tracks the language of healthy and unhealthy bodies across biology, ecology, fiction, and art. You can find him on Twitter at @hollowearths.

121: Erik Schurink is an exhibit designer, poet and sculptor. He participates in The Writhing Society and occasionally leads it. He is contributing artist to blog.abecedariumnyc.com, and Galerie de Difformité, which includes his *Do Not Eat This Book* chapbook. *Cryptozoo* is a journal in which he and eleven other writers respond to animalistic photographs he shot (Proteotypes, 2012). His *Homage to the Hum* (Métamatic Research Initiative) is due out in Spring 2014. He and his wife Rita host artist salons at their home and other intimate settings. Erik was born in the Netherlands and lives in Brooklyn, NY.

122: Theodora Ziolkowski's poems have appeared in *Prairie Schooner, Gargoyle Magazine,* and *Harpur Palate,* as well as an anthology of Vermont writers. She has a series of lyric poems forthcoming in an anthology of work inspired by the Demeter and Persephone myth.

123: Sarah Rubin holds a Master of Theological Studies from Harvard Divinity School and is a practicing Reiki master and Kripalu yoga teacher. She writes personal essays for her blog, sarahjrubin.com, and her writing has been featured on a number of other websites. Her love for poetry is a recent, and increasingly obsessive, development in her life.

124: Having received his MFA from the University of Colorado, Boulder, Jordan Windholz is currently a PhD candidate in early modern English literature at Fordham University. His dissertation examines representations of male singleness in the drama of Shakespeare and his contemporaries. His first collection of poems, *Other Psalms*, was selected by Averill Curdy for the 2014 Vassar Miller Prize in poetry.

It will be published by the University of North Texas Press in Spring 2015.

125: Professor Emeritus of English at Ohio Northern University, Claude Clayton Smith is the author of a novel, two children's books, four books of nonfiction, and a variety of poetry, plays, short fiction, and essays. His writing has been translated into five languages, including Russian and Chinese. His latest books are *Ohio Outback: Learning to Love the Great Black Swamp* (The Kent State University Press, 2010) and *The Way of Kinship: An Anthology of Native Siberian Literature* (The University of Minnesota Press, 2010), which he serves a co-editor/translator with the late Alexander Vaschenko of Moscow State University.

126: Matthew Hittinger is the author of *Skin Shift* (Sibling Rivalry Press, 2012) which earned him a nod on the *Poets & Writers Magazine* 8th Annual List of Debut Poets. His second collection, *The Erotic Postulate*, will be released in 2014, also from Sibling Rivalry Press. Matthew lives and works in New York City.

127: Jennifer Perrine is the author of *The Body Is No Machine* (New Issues, 2007), winner of the 2008 Devil's Kitchen Reading Award in Poetry, and *In the Human Zoo* (University of Utah Press, 2011), recipient of the 2010 Agha Shahid Ali Poetry Prize. Perrine teaches in the English department and directs the Women's and Gender Studies program at Drake University in Des Moines, Iowa.

128: Tom Merrill is Chair of the Department of Music and Theater, Assistant to the Dean for the Arts, and Director for Choral Activities at Xavier University, where he conducts the chamber choir, the Edgecliff Vocal Ensemble. He is the Director of Music at the Pleasant Ridge Presbyterian Church in Cincinnati and serves as the Vice-President of the American Choral Directors Association Central Division. He has served on the board of ChoralNet and is a past president of the Ohio Choral Directors Association. He is a board member of the Cincinnati Boy Choir.

129: Jehanne Dubrow is the author of four poetry collections, including most recently *Red Army Red* and *Stateside* (Northwestern University Press, 2012 and 2010). Her work has appeared in *Southern Review, The Hudson Review, Prairie Schooner,* and *Ploughshares.* She is the Director of the Rose O'Neill Literary House and Assistant Professor of Creative Writing at Washington College.

130: Antonio Vallone is Associate Professor of English at Penn State DuBois, publisher of MAMMOTH books (an independent literary press), and poetry editor of *Pennsylvania English*, published by the Pennsylvania College English Association, the state's branch of the College English Association. He has published several small press collections of poems: *The Blackbirds' Applause*, *Grass Saxophones*, *Chinese Bats*, and *Golden Carp*. Two collections are forthcoming: *American Zen* and *Blackberry Alleys: Collected Poems and Prose*.

131: Sarah Leavens holds an MFA in Poetry & Nonfiction from Chatham University and a BFA in Oil Painting from Wittenberg University. She was the 2012-2013 Out of the Forge Writer-in-Residence in Braddock, PA. With a background in public arts initiatives and outreach, she currently teaches visual art and writing at the Pittsburgh Center for the Arts and the University of Pittsburgh. Her recent work has appeared in *The Diverse Arts Press*, *Weave*, and *So to Speak*.

132: Eric Hack is a graduate student at Excelsior College in Albany, NY. He's a playwright, author, and graphic novelist. He takes little seriously other than the fun of words. Not really a hipster, but was uncool before uncool was cool.

133: Angelo Pastormerlo is currently working on translating/interpolating Allen Ginsberg's *Howl* into left-handed language (*Caw*). Somewhere along the way, Mr. Pastormerlo found the power to write a dashingly adequate people's history of Hubert's Dime Museum & Flea Circus, a subject on which he will be delivering a scared shitless lecture at the soon to be launched Morbid Anatomy Museum in Brooklyn sometime this year.

134: William Reichard is the author of four books of poetry, most recently *Sin Eater* (2010) and *This Brightness* (2007) both from Mid-List Press. He is the editor of the anthology *American Tensions: Literature of Identity and the Search for Social Justice* (New Village Press, 2011).

136: Will Stockton is Associate Professor of English at Clemson University and editor of *Upstart: A Journal of English Renaissance Studies*. He is the author of *Playing Dirty: Sexuality and Waste in Early Modern Comedy* (University of Minnesota Press, 2011) and co-editor of *Sex before Sex: Figuring the Act in Early Modern England* (University of Minnesota Press, 2013) and *Queer Renaissance Historiography: Backward Gaze* (Ashgate, 2009). With D. Gilson, he has authored a book of poems and essays entitled *Crush* (Punctum Books,

2014) and the chapbook *Gay Boys Write Straight Porn* (Sibling Rivalry Press, 2014). His poems have appeared in journals including *Assaracus*, *Bloom*, *Fourth River*, *PANK*, and *Weave*. Find him at willstockton.com.

137: Michael Basinski is the Curator of the Poetry Collection of the University Libraries, University at Buffalo. He performs his work as a solo poet and in ensemble with BuffFluxus. Among his recent books of poetry are *Piglittuce* (Propolis Press, 2013), *Learning Poem About Learning About Being A Poet* (Press Board Press, 2012) and *Trailers* (BlazeVox, 2011). His poems and other works have appeared in many magazines including *Dandelion, BoxKite, Antennae, Open Letter, Deluxe Rubber Chicken, First Offense, Terrible Work, Kenning, Lungfull, Tinfish, Score, Unarmed, Rampike, House Organ, Ferrum Wheel, End Note, Ur Vox, Damn the Caesars, Pilot, 1913, Filling Station, fhole, Public Illumination, Eccolinguistics, Western Humanities Review, Big Bridge, Mimeo Mimeo, Nerve Lantern, Vanitas, Talisman, Yellow Field, Staging Ground,* and *Poetry*. Recent visual opems (yes, opems) located at wordforword.info.

138: Moira Egan's poetry collections are *Cleave* (WWPH, 2004); *La Seta della Cravatta/The Silk of the Tie* (Edizioni l'Obliquo, 2009); *Bar Napkin Sonnets* (The Ledge Chapbook Competition, 2009); *Spin* (Entasis Press, 2010, for whom, with Clarinda Harriss, she also co-edited *Hot Sonnets*, 2011); and, most recently, *Hot Flash Sonnets* (Passager Books, 2013). Her poems and essays have appeared in numerous journals and anthologies in the U.S. and abroad, including *Best American Poetry 2008* and Lewis Turco's most recent edition of *The Book of Forms*. With Damiano Abeni, she has published more than a dozen books in translation, by authors such as Barth, Bender, Ferlinghetti, Hecht, Strand, Tey, and John Ashbery, whose collection, *Un mondo che non può essere migliore: Poesie scelte 1956-2007,* won a Special Prize of the Premio Napoli (2009). She has been a Mid Atlantic Arts Fellow at the Virginia Center for the Creative Arts; Writer in Residence at St. James Cavalier Centre for Creativity, Malta; a Writing Fellow at the Civitella Ranieri Center; and a Fellow at the Rockefeller Foundation Bellagio Center. She lives in Rome, and teaches literature and creative writing.

139: Mark Cugini is the author of *I'm Just Happy To Be Here* (Ink Press, 2014). His work has appeared or is forthcoming in *Melville House, Hobart, Sink Review, Fanzine, NOÖ, Everday Genius* (6x), and other publications. He's a founding editor of *Big Lucks*, a workshop instructor at The Writer's Center in Washington, DC, and a recipient of a Scholarship Grant to the Juniper Summer Writing Institute at UMass Amherst. In 2013, he was named one of the Top 200 Advocates of American Poetry by *The Huffington Post.*

140: Neal Whitman took up writing general poetry in 2005 with now over 200 poems published and haiku in 2008 with over 400 in publication. He and his wife, Elaine, combine his poetry with her Native American flute in recital.

141: Daniel Zender is a freelance illustrator and designer, living and working in Brooklyn, NY. His clients include the *NY Times, LA Times, Boston Globe, McSweeney's, Progressive, Nautilus,* and*Flaunt.* See more at danielzender.com.

142: Maggie O'Connor owns a bookstore in Eureka Springs, Arkansas. Her one woman show, *Mrs. Dalloway Goes to Dixie,* is currently playing in Los Angeles.

143: Alexandra Edelblute earned her master's degree in English at the University at Buffalo, where — as a student of the poetics program — she focused on the theory, practice, and textual study of poetry. She writes creative nonfiction and poetry; her work has appeared in *Smartish Pace.*

144: Ross McCleary enjoys experimenting with language and form. He lives and writes in Edinburgh, Scotland.

145: Andy Decker received his MFA in Pittsburgh, PA, where he teaches English as a Second Language (ESL).

146: Caroline Tanski is a writer, editor, and former library assistant who lives in Boston, Massachusetts. She earned her MFA from Chatham University and writes about her mother with alarming frequency.

147: Lisa Ampleman is the author of a book of poetry, *Full Cry* (NFSPS Press, 2013), and a chapbook,*I've Been Collecting This to Tell You* (Kent State University Press, 2012). Her poems have appeared or are forthcoming in journals such as *Poetry, Kenyon Review Online, 32 Poems,* and on Poetry Daily and Verse Daily.

148: Dianne Berg is a doctoral candidate in the Tufts University English department. She's interested in transgressive female language and behavior, and her dissertation examines popular literary representations of sensational "real life" cases of domestic violence in 16th & 17th

Century England. Before graduate school, Dianne was the education program manager at a medieval and Renaissance armor museum.

149: Chris Emslie is assistant editor at *ILK Journal*. His poems have appeared or are forthcoming in *Anti-, Whiskey Island* & *PANK*, among others. He lives in Tuscaloosa, where he is an MFA candidate at the University of Alabama & a recent convert to roadside bodegas.

150: Jennifer Franklin holds an MFA from Columbia University. She was featured in *The Paris Review*'s "Ten New Poets" issue and her chapbook, *Persephone's Ransom*, is available from Finishing Line Press.

151: Kevin Barton earned his MFA in photography from the Rhode Island School of Design. Originally from Salt Lake City, he currently lives in Boston working at Harvard University. His work largely explores spaces, activities, and rituals that are rooted in what he describes as prescribed happiness or enforced fun. He loves collecting, working with archives, photographs of all kinds, and has an odd yet charming love of snails. More of his work can be seen at kevinbartonphoto.com.

152: Jennifer Murvin's essays and stories have appeared in *The Sun, The Cincinnati Review, Mid-American Review, Bellingham Review, Midwestern Gothic, Baltimore Review, Revolver*, and *Huizache*, among others. She teaches writing at Missouri State University and holds an MFA from Pacific University. For more of Jen's writing, please visit jennifermurvin.virb.com.

153: Pamela Allen Brown lives in Brooklyn, New York, and works as an Associate Professor of English at the University of Connecticut. Her poems have appeared in *Ep;phany, Public, Frontier*, and *R/rose*, and her one-act plays have been performed in New York and Boston. Her scholarly publications include *Better a Shrew than a Sheep: Women, Drama, and the Culture of Jest in Early Modern England; As You Like It: Texts and Contexts* (co-edited with Jean Howard); and *Women Players in England, 1500-1660: Beyond the All-Male Stage* (co-edited with Peter Parolin). Currently she is working on *Boying Her Grandezza: Shakespeare and the Italian Diva* and a collaborative translation of Isabella Andreini's stage dialogues.

154: Wayne Koestenbaum is a Distinguished Professor of English at the City University of New York's Graduate Center. His latest book is *My 1980s & Other Essays* (Farrar, Straus and Giroux, 2013).

About the Editor

D. Gilson is the author of *I Will Say This Exactly One Time: Essays* (Sibling Rivalry, 2015); *Crush* with Will Stockton (Punctum Books, 2014); *Brit Lit* (Sibling Rivalry, 2013); and *Catch & Release* (2012), winner of the Robin Becker Prize. He is Assistant Professor of English at Massachusetts College of Liberal Arts, and his work has appeared in *PANK, The Indiana Review, The Rumpus*, and as a notable essay in *Best American Essays*.

www.ingramcontent.com/pod-product-compliance
Lightning Source LLC
Chambersburg PA
CBHW021853230426
43671CB00006B/377